"Breit" QUILTS
to Appliqué

LEISURE ARTS, INC.
Little Rock, Arkansas

EDITORIAL STAFF

Vice President and Editor-in-Chief: Sandra Graham Case.
Executive Director of Publications: Cheryl Nodine Gunnells.
Senior Publications Director: Susan White Sullivan.
Publications Operations Director: Cheryl Johnson.
Senior Art Operations Director: Jeff Curtis.
Licensed Product Coordinator: Lisa Truxton Curton.
Senior Director of Public Relations and Retail Marketing:
    Stephen Wilson.

TECHNICAL

Leaflet Publications Director: Mary Sullivan Hutcheson.
Senior Technical Editor: Lisa Lancaster.
Technical Writer: Andrea Ahlen.

DESIGN

Designer: Linda Diehl Tiano.

EDITORIAL

Associate Editor: Kimberly L. Ross.

ART

Art Publications Director: Rhonda Shelby.
Art Imaging Director: Mark Hawkins.
Art Category Manager: Lora Puls.
Graphic Artist: Jenny Dickerson.
Publishing Systems Administrator: Becky Riddle.
Publishing Systems Assistants: Clint Hanson, John Rose,
    and Chris Wertenberger.
Photography Stylists: Karen Hall, Cassie Newsome,
    and Janna Laughlin.

BUSINESS STAFF

Publisher: Rick Barton.
Vice President, Finance: Tom Siebenmorgen.
Director of Corporate Planning and Development:
    Laticia Mull Dittrich.
Vice President, Retail Marketing: Bob Humphrey.
Vice President, Sales: Ray Shelgosh.
Vice President, National Accounts: Pam Stebbins.
Director of Sales and Services: Margaret Reinold.
Vice President, Operations: Jim Dittrich.
Comptroller, Operations: Rob Thieme.
Retail Customer Service Manager: Stan Raynor.
Print Production Manager: Fred F. Pruss.

Sow good services; sweet remembrances will grow from them.
Mde. de Stael

Made in the United States of America.

Softcover ISBN 1-57486-439-4

10 9 8 7 6 5 4 3 2 1

"Breit" QUILT
to Appliqué

FOR THE CUTEST QUILTED CREATIONS EVER, turn to the Queen of Everything, MARY ENGELBREIT!

Choose from 23 projects, each one based on Mary's most enchanting artwork. Easy-to-follow patterns and unforgettable photographs make it oh-so simple to transform a sewing room, garden room, and little princess's bedroom into a magical "Mary-land."

Or add a touch of fun to an empty nook or cranny with two whimsical wall hangings. No matter what you choose, you're sure to cherish these charming designs!

Table of CONTENTS

Mary ENGELBREIT

photo by Rich Saal

Growing up in St. Louis, Missouri, Mary Engelbreit adored drawing. She began sketching as soon as she could hold a crayon, teaching herself first by copying the work of classic children's illustrators like Jessie Wilcox Smith and Johnny Gruelle, the creator of Raggedy Ann and Raggedy Andy. At age 8, Mary started drawing original artwork, often to accompany a story or book that she was reading. Before long, she had her first "studio" — a hastily vacated linen closet.

"We jammed a desk and chair in there, and I'm sure it was 110 degrees," Mary laughs. "But I would happily sit in that closet for hours at a time and draw pictures."

Her passion for drawing continued to grow, and by the age of 11, Mary knew without a doubt that she wanted to grow up to be an artist. She got her start during high school, selling hand-drawn greeting cards at a local store for 25 cents, then 50 cents. But the nuns at her Catholic high school discouraged her from becoming an artist, saying it wasn't a practical way to make a living. After graduation, Mary worked for almost two years at an art supply store, where she met a number of professional artists who changed her perspective on the business.

"It was a big wake-up call," Mary remembers. "I realized I could live my dream."

After short-lived careers at an ad agency and the St. Louis Post-Dispatch, Mary began working as a free-lance illustrator. In 1977 she married Phil Delano, a social worker, and with his support, Mary started illustrating fantasy greeting cards, depicting dragons, unicorns, castles, and the like. But Mary's style underwent a significant change when her first son was born in 1980.

"Fantasy went out the window, and I began to illustrate reality — there was so much inspiration around me," Mary says. "Suddenly everyday life seemed more interesting to me. I figured that since we probably lived the same kind of life that everyone else seemed to be living, these things must be interesting to them, too."

At this time, Mary began honing her own distinctive style: a richly detailed, nostalgic mixture of whimsical and profound quotes, precocious children like her alter-ego, Ann Estelle, and, of course, her trademark cherries and Scottie dogs.

As Mary found her niche, she decided the time was ripe to start her own greeting card company. She took 12 designs to the National Stationery Show in New York and was thrilled to discover that her work was a hit. A big hit, in fact: by 1986, just three years after her first showing, Mary's greeting card company was making a million dollars a year.

With the incredible reception her art was receiving, Mary took a cue from a fan and chose to license her greeting cards and expand the arena in which her artwork was available. "I always like to share the story of a fan who once told me she wished she could live in my greeting cards. Many fans have written similar letters — that they want to make their homes look like my drawings," Mary confesses.

Now an internationally known artist, Mary has created more than 4,000 images that are featured in her award-winning magazine and on a variety of merchandise, including an exclusive line of craft books and leaflets from industry leader Leisure Arts.

But according to Mary, although success is sweet, the ability to spend her days drawing is far better.

"I know it's ridiculous, but I think, 'What do people do if they don't draw?' " she admits. "I have always believed if you choose a job you love, you'll never work a day in your life … and to be able to make a living from drawing — I just can't describe what it's like. It's the most satisfying thing I can possibly think of doing. I'm just so fortunate."

Princess of Quite-A-Lot
BEDROOM

Every little princess deserves a fairy-tale abode — and pretty shades of pink combine with playful posies to make these royal chambers just such a place. Winsome pillows top fanciful bedding, while an enchanting vanity holds her trinkets and treasures. A wall hanging, basket liner, and tote bag complete this magical room.

TOO MUCH OF A GOOD THING
IS WONDERFUL

MAE WEST

Trimmed in fashionable eyelash fringe and filled with some of her favorite things, this endearing **TOTE BAG** will make your little princess feel all grown-up.

A white wicker basket and a charming **BASKET LINER** make a wonderful caddy for stationery and more.

Pom-poms and precious "jewels" adorn an adorable **CROWN PILLOW**, while ribbons, lace, and other fancy frills make a **BORDER PILLOW** and a **BOLSTER PILLOW** even prettier.

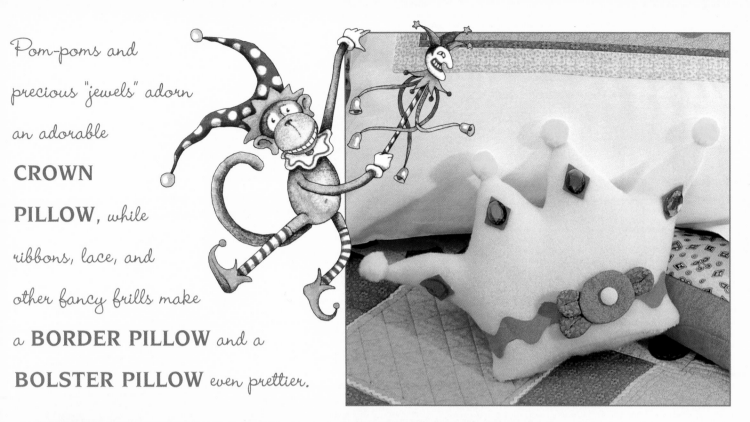

Covered in beautiful blooms, this Princess of Quite-A-Lot

QUILT, with matching Princess **PILLOWCASE** and **SHEET**,

is just right for the royal bedroom. A coordinating Princess of

Quite-A-Lot **WALL HANGING** (pictured on page 10) and

VANITY TABLE and **SEAT** add a little something extra

to the regal theme.

Princess of Quite·A·Lot Quilt

FINISHED BLOCK SIZE: 8" x 8" (20 cm x 20 cm)
FINISHED QUILT SIZE: 65" x 87" (165 cm x 221 cm)

YARDAGE REQUIREMENTS

Yardage is based on 45" (114 cm) wide fabric.

$5/8$ yd (57 cm) **each** of light and medium pink print fabrics for blocks

2 yds (1.8 m) of dark pink print fabric for flower appliqués and inner border

$1^1/4$ yds (1.1 m) of yellow floral print fabric for flower block backgrounds

$2^1/4$ yds (2.1 m) of yellow novelty print fabric for middle border

Scrap of yellow solid fabric for flower center appliqués

$2^3/8$ yds (2.2 m) of green print fabric for leaf appliqués, sashings, and outer border

$5/8$ yd (57 cm) of binding fabric

$5^3/8$ yds (4.9 m) of backing fabric

73" x 95" (1.9 m x 2.4 m) batting

You will also need:

Paper-backed fusible web

1 yd (91 cm) of fusible interfacing

Stabilizer

$18^5/8$ yds (17.0 m) of canary baby rickrack

CUTTING OUT THE BLOCKS AND BORDERS

*Follow **Rotary Cutting**, page 83, to cut fabric. All measurements include a $1/4$" seam allowance. Measurements for flower block background squares include an extra 2". Trim to correct size after appliquéing. Cutting lengths given for borders are exact. You may wish to add an extra 2" of length at each end for "insurance," trimming borders to fit quilt top center.*

From light pink print fabric:
- Cut 2 strips $8^1/2$" wide. From these strips, cut 8 squares (**A**) $8^1/2$" x $8^1/2$".

From medium pink print fabric:
- Cut 2 strips $8^1/2$" wide. From these strips, cut 7 squares (**B**) $8^1/2$" x $8^1/2$".

From dark pink print fabric:
- Cut 2 lengthwise inner side borders (**C**) $6^1/2$" x $58^1/2$".
- Cut 2 lengthwise inner top/bottom borders (**D**) $6^1/2$" x $48^1/2$".

From yellow floral print fabric:
- Cut 5 strips $7^1/2$" wide. From these strips, cut 24 squares (**E**) $7^1/2$" x $7^1/2$" for flower block backgrounds.

From yellow novelty print fabric:
- Cut 2 lengthwise middle side borders (**F**) $3^1/2$" x $70^1/2$".
- Cut 2 lengthwise middle top/bottom borders (**G**) $3^1/2$" x $54^1/2$".

From green print fabric:
- Cut 2 lengthwise outer side borders (**H**) $5^1/2$" x $76^1/2$".
- Cut 2 lengthwise outer top/bottom borders (**I**) $5^1/2$" x $64^1/2$".

From remaining width:
- Cut 20 sashing strips (**J**) $3^1/2$" x $8^1/2$".
- Cut 6 sashing strips (**K**) $3^1/2$" x $36^1/2$".

From binding fabric:
- Cut 8 strips $2^1/2$" wide.

From fusible interfacing:
- Cut 24 squares (**L**) $5^1/2$" x $5^1/2$".

CUTTING OUT THE APPLIQUÉS

*Appliqué patterns, pages 17-18, do not include seam allowances and are reversed. Follow **Preparing Fusible Appliqué Pieces**, page 85, to cut out appliqués.*

From green print fabric:
- Use pattern to cut 96 leaves (**a**).

From dark pink fabric:
- Use pattern to cut 24 flowers (**b**).

From yellow solid fabric:
- Use pattern to cut 24 flower centers (**c**).

MAKING THE FLOWER BLOCKS

*Follow **Machine Appliqué**, page 85, to make flower blocks. Refer to **Block Diagram** and photo, page 8, for placement.*

1. Position 4 leaves (**a**), 1 flower (**b**), and 1 flower center (**c**) on a yellow floral print square (**E**) and fuse in place.
2. Appliqué pieces using matching thread and a Satin Stitch to make **Flower Block**. Trim block to measure 5¹/₂" x 5¹/₂". Make 24 **Flower Blocks**.

Flower Block
(make 24)

3. Matching right side of **Flower Block** and fusible side of an interfacing square (**L**), sew block and interfacing together around all edges. Cut a small slit in the center of interfacing and turn block right side out, finger pressing edges. Repeat for all blocks.

ASSEMBLING THE QUILT TOP

*Refer to **Piecing** and **Pressing**, page 84, and **Quilt Top Diagram**, page 18, to make the quilt top. Use a ¹/₄" seam allowance for all seams.*

1. Sew 2 light pink squares (**A**), 1 medium pink square (**B**), and 4 sashing strips (**J**) together as shown to make **Row 1**. Make 3 **Row 1's**.
2. Sew 1 light pink square (**A**), 2 medium pink squares (**B**), and 4 sashing strips (**J**) together as shown to make **Row 2**. Make 2 **Row 2's**.
3. Sew 6 sashing strips (**K**) and **Rows 1** and **2** together as shown to make **Quilt Top Center**.

ADDING THE BORDERS

*Refer to **Quilt Top Diagram**, page 18, to add the borders. Match centers and corners and ease in fullness on all borders.*

1. Sew inner side borders (**C**), then inner top/bottom borders (**D**) to **Quilt Top Center**.
2. Sew middle side borders (**F**), then middle top/bottom borders (**G**) to pieced center.
3. Sew outer side borders (**H**), then outer top/bottom borders (**I**) to pieced center.

COMPLETING THE QUILT

Refer to photo, page 8, for placement.

1. Sew rickrack around edges of squares (**A** and **B**) and outer edges of **Quilt Top Center**.
2. Position **Flower Blocks** on quilt top as shown and fuse in place. Using matching thread, topstitch close to edge of blocks.
3. Follow **Quilting**, page 86, to mark, layer, and quilt as desired. Our quilt was machine quilted.
4. Follow **Making Straight Grain Binding**, page 91, to make 8³/₄ yds of 2¹/₂"w binding.
5. Follow **Attaching Binding with Mitered Corners**, page 91, to attach binding to quilt.

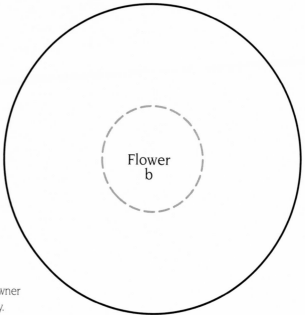

Flower
b

Quilt Top Diagram

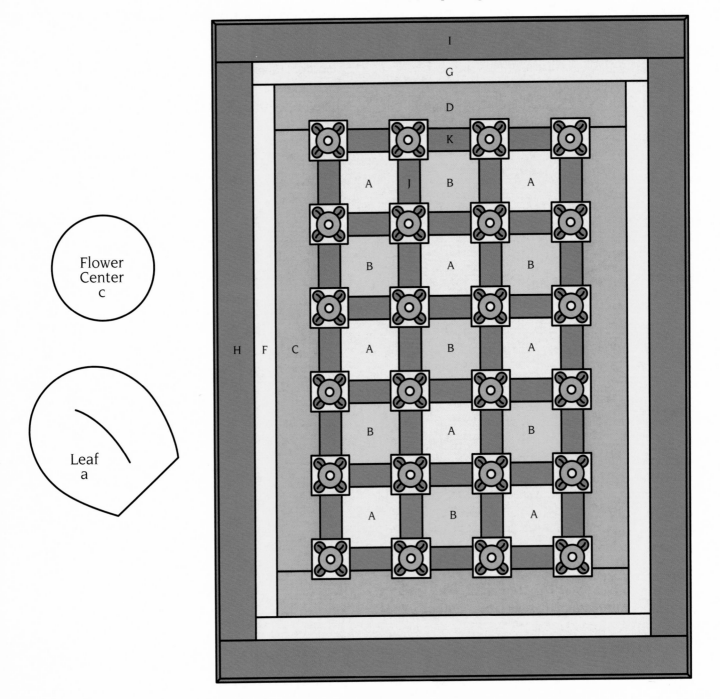

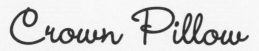

Crown Pillow

FINISHED SIZE: 13" x 8½" (33 cm x 22 cm)

YARDAGE REQUIREMENTS:

Yardage is based on 45" (114 cm) wide fabric.

⅜ yd (34 cm) of yellow fleece
Scrap of pink fleece
Scraps of dark pink print, yellow solid, and
  green print fabrics for flower

You will also need:

Fabric glue
Freezer paper
Plush felt
Polyester fiberfill
½ yd (46 cm) of 1⅛" (29 mm) wide dark pink
  rickrack
One ⅜" (10 mm) diameter button from covered
  button kit
Four assorted 25 mm x 18 mm oval low dome
  stones
Four 1" (25 mm) diameter yellow pompoms

MAKING THE PILLOW

Match right sides and use a ¼" seam allowance for all seams.

1. Using pattern, pages 20-21, cut 2 crowns (**A**) from yellow fleece and sew together around sides and top. Turn crown right side out and stuff with fiberfill.

2. Using pattern, cut 1 crown base (**B**) from yellow fleece and sew to bottom of crown.

3. Position dark pink rickrack around crown 1" from bottom edge; glue in place.

4. Glue a pompom to each point of crown.

5. Using pattern, cut 4 diamonds (**C**) from pink fleece. Glue a stone to each diamond. Glue diamonds to crown.

6. Using pattern, trace flower (**D**) onto the dull side of freezer paper. Iron freezer paper, shiny side down, onto wrong side of fabric piece. Matching right sides and raw edges, place a second fabric piece underneath. Stitch around entire flower pattern. Peel off freezer paper, and trim flower close to stitching. Cut slit on 1 side of flower to turn. Cut a piece of plush felt slightly smaller than flower pattern. Turn flower right side out and insert plush felt; whipstitch slit closed. Follow manufacturer's instructions to cover button with yellow fabric. Sew button to center of flower, going through both layers of flower. Make 3 leaves (**E**) in the same manner, but leave flat end open for turning. Turn and sew short seam on each leaf for center vein.

7. Glue leaves and flower to crown.

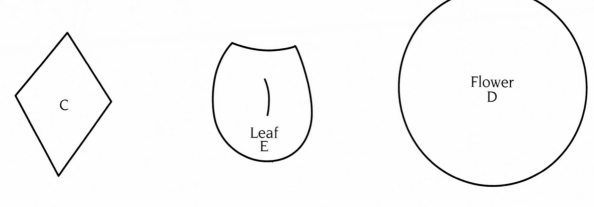

C

Leaf
E

Flower
D

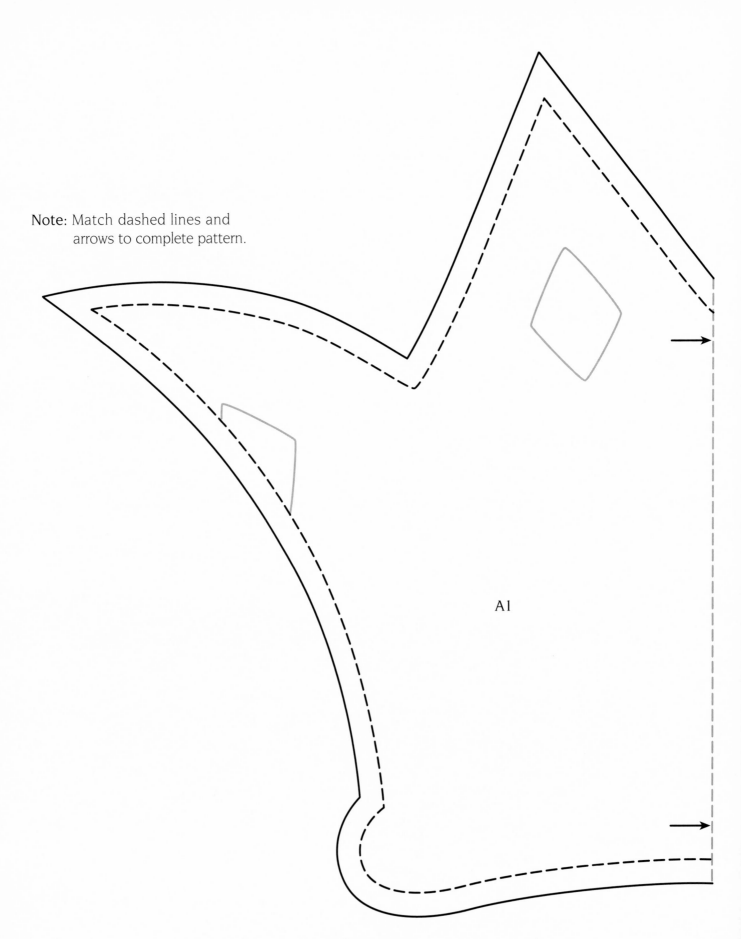

Note: Match dashed lines and arrows to complete pattern.

A1

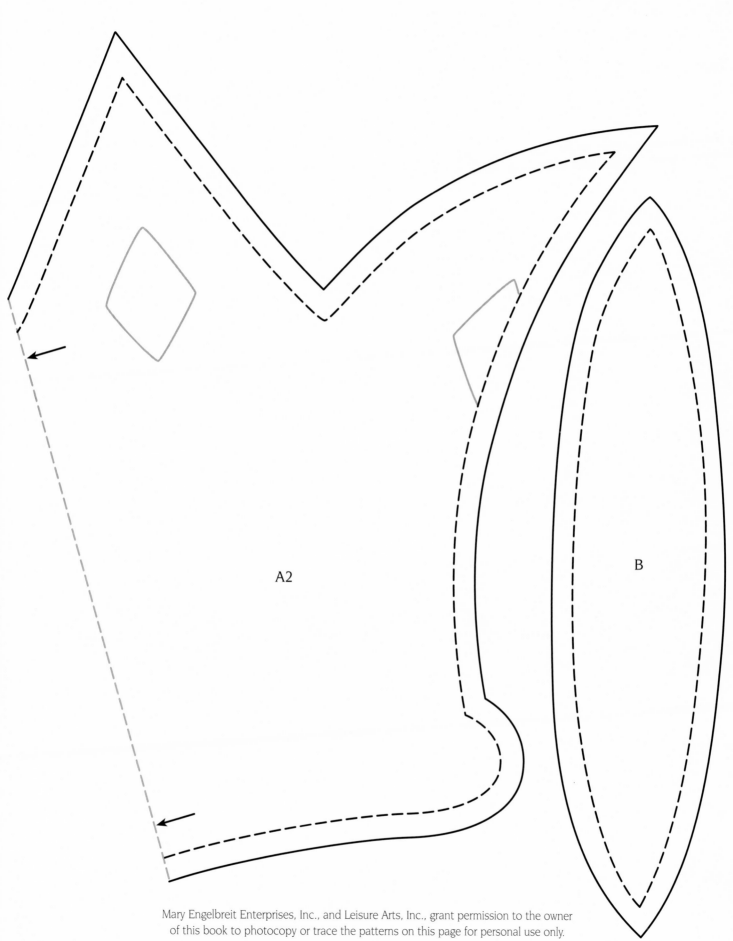

A2

B

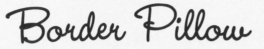

Border Pillow

FINISHED SIZE: 16" x 16" (41 cm x 41 cm)

YARDAGE REQUIREMENTS

Yardage is based on 45" (114 cm) wide fabric.

Scrap of yellow print fabric

$^1/_8$ yd (11 cm) of green print fabric

$^5/_8$ yd (57 cm) of light pink print fabric for border and backing

Scraps of dark pink print and yellow solid fabric for flower appliqué

You will also need:

Paper-backed fusible web

Stabilizer

$^7/_8$ yd (80 cm) of white medium rickrack

$1^1/_4$ yds (1.1 m) of white jumbo rickrack

$1^1/_4$ yds (1.1 m) of $^5/_8$" (57 cm) wide checked ribbon

2 yds (1.8 m) of light pink $^1/_2$" (13 mm) diameter ball fringe

2 yds (1.8 m) of $1^1/_2$" (38 mm) wide white eyelet

Four $^7/_8$" (22 mm) diameter buttons from covered button kit

$^3/_4$ yd (69 cm) of $^3/_8$" (10 mm) wide mint green satin ribbon

Fabric glue

16" x 16" (41 cm x 41 cm) square pillow form

CUTTING OUT THE PIECES

Appliqué patterns, page 23, do not include seam allowances and are reversed. Use a $^1/_4$" seam allowance unless otherwise indicated. Measurements for background square include an extra 2". Trim to correct size after appliquéing.

From yellow print fabric:

- Cut 1 background square (A) $9^1/_2$" x $9^1/_2$".

From green print fabric:

- Cut 2 inner side borders (B) $1^1/_2$" x $7^1/_2$".
- Cut 2 inner top/bottom borders (C) $1^1/_2$" x $9^1/_2$".

From light pink print fabric:

- Cut 2 outer side borders (D) $4^1/_4$" x $9^1/_2$".
- Cut 2 outer top/bottom borders (E) $4^1/_4$" x 17".
- Cut 2 backing rectangles (F) 10" x 17"

From dark pink, yellow solid, and green fabrics:

- Cut 1 leaf (a), 2 leaves (b), 1 flower (c), and 1 flower center (d).

MAKING THE PILLOW

*Follow **Machine Appliqué**, page 85, to make the pillow. Refer to photo, page 13, for placement.*

1. Position 1 leaf (a), 2 leaves (b), 1 flower (c), and 1 flower center (d) on yellow print square (A) and fuse in place. Appliqué pieces using Satin Stitch and matching thread. Trim block to measure $7^1/_2$" x $7^1/_2$".

2. Cut four $6^1/_2$" lengths of white medium rickrack. Position rickrack $^1/_2$" from raw edges of center block and topstitch in place using matching thread.

3. Sew 2 green inner side borders (B), then 2 green inner top/bottom borders (C) to pillow top center.

4. Sew 2 light pink outer side borders (D), then 2 light pink outer top/bottom borders (E) to pieced center.

5. Baste jumbo white rickrack to 1 edge of checked ribbon. Beginning at 1 corner and mitering corners, pin remaining edge of ribbon along edge of seam between the inner and outer borders. Topstitch ribbon in place along both edges using matching thread.

6. Matching straight edges, position pink ball fringe on top of eyelet trim; baste together. Matching right sides and raw edges, baste trim to pillow top.

7. For button flowers, follow manufacturer's instructions to cover 4 buttons with light pink print fabric. Cut four $3/8$" diameter circles from yellow fabric and glue to center of each covered button. For leaves, cut eight 3" lengths of green satin ribbon. Matching cut ends, fold ribbon in half, forming a point (**Fig. 1**). Glue cut ends together to make a ribbon leaf. Glue 2 ribbon leaves to wrong side of each covered button. Sew buttons to each corner of pillow center, covering rickrack corners.

Fig. 1

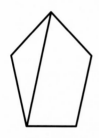

8. Sew a $1/4$" hem (turned under twice) on one long edge of each backing rectangle (**F**). Matching right sides and raw edges, place pillow backs on pillow front, overlapping finished edges of backs at center. Using a $1/2$" **seam allowance**, sew pillow front and backs together. Turn pillow right side out and insert pillow form.

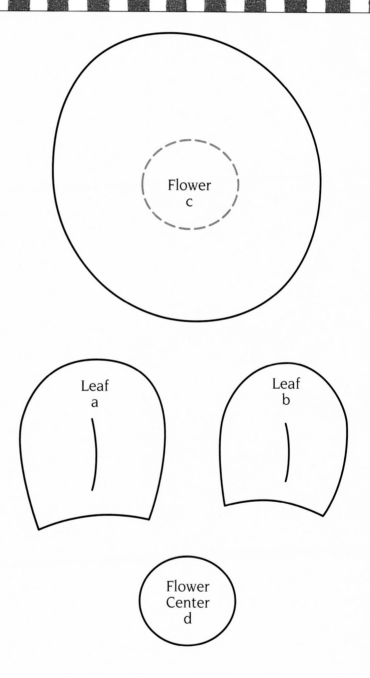

Flower
c

Leaf
a

Leaf
b

Flower
Center
d

Bolster Pillow

FINISHED SIZE: 6" x 15" (15 cm x 38 cm)

YARDAGE REQUIREMENTS

Yardage is based on 45" (114 cm) wide fabric.

Scraps of yellow floral print, dark pink print, and yellow solid fabrics

18" x 22" (46 cm x 56 cm) piece of medium pink print fabric

$^1/_8$ yd (11 cm) of green print fabric

$^3/_8$ yd (34 cm) of yellow print fabric

You will also need:

Paper-backed fusible web

Stabilizer

Fusible interfacing

$^3/_4$ yd (69 cm) of white medium rickrack

$2^1/_4$ yds (2.1 m) of 1" (25 mm) wide white eyelet

$1^1/_8$ yds (1.0 m) of $^5/_8$" (16 mm) wide checked ribbon

$1^3/_4$ yds (1.6 m) of $^5/_8$" (16 mm) wide white ribbon

6" x 15" (15 cm x 38 cm) bolster pillow form

CUTTING OUT THE PIECES

Appliqué patterns, page 23, do not include seam allowance and are reversed. Use a $^1/_4$" seam allowance unless otherwise indicated. Measurements for background square include an extra 2". Trim to correct size after appliquéing.

From yellow floral print fabric:

- Cut 1 background square (**A**) $8^1/_2$" x $8^1/_2$".

From medium pink print fabric:

- Cut 1 rectangle (**B**) $9^1/_2$" x 19".

From green print fabric:

- Cut 2 strips (**C**) $1^1/_2$" x 19".

From yellow print fabric:

- Cut 2 rectangles (**D**) 9" x 19".

From dark pink, yellow solid, and green fabrics for appliqués:

- Cut 1 leaf (**a**), 2 leaves (**b**), 1 flower (**c**), and 1 flower center (**d**).

From fusible interfacing:

- Cut 1 square (**E**) $6^1/_2$" x $6^1/_2$".

MAKING THE PILLOW

*Follow **Machine Appliqué**, page 85, to make the pillow. Refer to photo for placement.*

1. Position 1 leaf (**a**), 2 leaves (**b**), 1 flower (**c**), and 1 flower center (**d**) on a yellow print square (**A**) and fuse in place. Appliqué pieces using Satin Stitch and matching thread. Centering appliqué, trim block to measure $6^1/_2$" x $6^1/_2$".

2. Matching right side of flower block and fusible side of interfacing square (**E**), sew block and interfacing together. Cut a small slit in the center of interfacing and turn block right side out, finger pressing edges. Position flower block on center of medium pink rectangle (**B**) and fuse in place. Center rickrack over edge of flower block and topstitch in place using matching thread.

3. Cut four 19" lengths of eyelet; set 2 aside. Matching straight edge and wrong side of one 19" length of eyelet to right side of long edge of center section; baste eyelet in place. Repeat for other long edge.

4. Cut two 19" lengths of checked ribbon. Center 1 ribbon on each green print strip (**C**) and topstitch in place. Matching right sides and long edges, sew a green print strip to each side of center section.

5. Sew a $^1/_4$" hem (turned under twice) on one long edge of yellow print rectangle (**D**). Matching straight edge and wrong side of one 19" length of eyelet to remaining long edge; baste eyelet in place. Repeat for other yellow print rectangle.

6. Matching right sides and raw edges, sew a yellow print rectangle to each green print strip.

7. Cut two 30" lengths of white ribbon. With right sides together and matching raw edges, fold pillow top in half and stitch using a $^1/_2$" **seam allowance**. Turn pillow right side out and insert pillow form. Referring to photo, tie a length of ribbon in a bow around each end of pillow.

Tote Bag
FINISHED SIZE: 8¹/₂" x 9" (22 cm x 23 cm)

YARDAGE REQUIREMENTS
Yardage is based on 45" (114 cm) wide fabric.

   18" x 22" (46 cm x 56 cm) piece **each** of light
   pink, dark pink, yellow, and green print fabrics

You will also need:

   ⁵/₈ yd (57 cm) **each** of ⁵/₈" (15.9 mm) wide canary
   and emerald jumbo rickrack

   ⁵/₈ yd (57 cm) of 2" (50.8 mm) wide pink eyelash
   fringe

CUTTING OUT THE PIECES
All measurements include a ¹/₂" seam allowance.

From light pink print fabric:
* Cut 2 rectangles (A) 9¹/₂" x 2¹/₂".
* Cut 1 lining piece (B) 9¹/₂" x 21".

From green print fabric:
* Cut 2 rectangles (C) 9¹/₂" x 2".
* Cut 2 rectangles (D) 3" x 15" for handles.

From yellow print fabric:
* Cut 2 rectangles (E) 9¹/₂" x 4¹/₂".

From dark pink print fabric:
* Cut 1 rectangle (F) 9¹/₂" x 9".

MAKING THE TOTE
*Match right sides and raw edges and use a ¹/₂" seam
allowance for all seams.*

1. Matching long edges, sew each light pink print
    rectangle (**A**) and green print rectangle (C)
    together to make 2 top sections. Center a 9¹/₂"
    length of canary rickrack over each seam and
    sew in place.
2. Matching straight edge of fringe and 1 long
    edge of yellow rectangle, baste a 9¹/₂" length of
    pink eyelash fringe to right side of each yellow
    print rectangle (E) to make 2 middle sections.
3. Matching remaining long edge of green print
    rectangle (C) and fringed edge of yellow print
    rectangle (E), sew each top section to a
    middle section.

4. Matching remaining long edge of each middle
    section and short edges of dark pink print
    rectangle (F), sew pieced top and middle
    sections to tote bottom.
5. Center a 9¹/₂" length of emerald rickrack over
    each middle/bottom seam; sew in place.
6. Matching right sides and top edges, fold tote in
    half. Pin side edges together and sew. Repeat
    for tote lining (**B**).
7. To make boxed corners in tote, match each side
    seam to center fold of bottom section. Sew
    across each corner 1¹/₂" from end (**Fig. 1**).
    Repeat for tote lining (**B**). Do not turn lining
    right side out.

Fig. 1

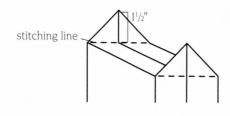

stitching line — 1¹/₂"

8. For handles, fold each green print rectangle
    (**D**) in half lengthwise; sew long edges
    together. Turn handles right side out.
    Centering seam in back; press. Pin ends of 1
    handle to right side of tote front 1" from side
    seams. Repeat for remaining handle and tote
    back. Baste handles in place.
9. Matching right sides and top edges, place tote
    inside lining. Sew lining and tote together along
    top edge, leaving an opening for turning. Turn
    tote right side out and press. Topstitch close to
    top edge of tote.

Princess of Quite·A·Lot Wall Hanging

FINISHED SIZE: 27¹/₄" x 17" (69 cm x 43 cm)

YARDAGE REQUIREMENTS

Yardage is based on 45" (114 cm) wide fabric.

¹/₄ yd (23 cm) **each** of dark pink, medium pink, light pink, and green print fabrics

¹/₈ yd (11 cm) of yellow print fabric

Scraps of black, dark green, and yellow solid fabrics for appliqués

¹/₄ yd (23 cm) of binding fabric

³/₄ yd (69 cm) of fabric for backing and hanging sleeve

35" x 25" (89 cm x 64 cm) batting

You will also need:

Paper-backed fusible web

Stabilizer

2 yds (1.8 m) of 1" (25 mm) wide white eyelet

Embroidery floss — white

Tracing paper

Fabric-marking pencil

CUTTING OUT THE PIECES

Follow **Piecing** *and* **Pressing***, page 84, and* **Preparing Fusible Appliqué Pieces***, page 85, to cut fabric. Appliqué patterns, pages 27 and 29-30, do not include seam allowances and are reversed. All measurements include a* ¹/₄" *seam allowance.*

From medium pink print fabric:

*   Cut 1 background rectangle (**A**) 18¹/₄" x 8".

From dark pink print fabric for appliqués:

*   Use patterns to cut letters.
*   Use pattern to cut 3 flowers (**c**).

From yellow print fabric:

*   Cut 2 inner side borders (**B**) 1¹/₄" x 8".
*   Cut 2 inner top/bottom borders (**C**) 1¹/₄" x 19³/₄".

From light pink print fabric:

*   Cut 2 middle side borders (**D**) 2" x 9¹/₂".
*   Cut 2 middle top/bottom borders (**E**) 2" x 22³/₄".

From green print fabric:

*   Cut 2 outer side borders (**F**) 2¹/₂" x 12¹/₂".
*   Cut 2 outer top/bottom borders (**G**) 2¹/₂" x 26³/₄".
*   Use pattern to cut 1 large oval (**e**).

From black solid fabric for appliqués:

*   Use pattern to cut 1 small oval (**f**).

From dark green solid fabric for appliqués:

*   Use patterns to cut 6 leaves (**a**) and 2 leaves (**b**).

From yellow solid fabric for appliqués:

*   Use pattern to cut 3 flower centers (**d**).

From binding fabric:

*   Cut 3 strips 2¹/₂" wide.

MAKING THE WALL HANGING TOP

Refer to photo, page 10, for placement. Use ¹/₄" seam allowance for all seams.

1. Position letters, "PRINCESS OF QUITE·A·LOT," on medium pink print background rectangle (**A**) and fuse in place.
2. Sew 2 inner side borders (**B**), then 2 inner top/bottom borders (**C**) to wall hanging center.
3. Sew 2 middle side borders (**D**), then 2 middle top/bottom borders (**E**) to pieced center.
4. Matching raw edges and wrong side of eyelet to right side of middle border, baste a 12¹/₂" length of eyelet to each side border, then a 22³/₄" length to top/bottom borders.
5. Sew 2 outer borders (**F**) to sides, then 2 outer borders (**G**) to top and bottom of wall hanging center.
6. Position leaves (**a** and **b**), flowers (**c**), flower centers (**d**), green print large oval (**e**) and black solid small oval (**f**), and letters, "THE," on upper left corner of wall hanging. Fuse in place.

COMPLETING THE WALL HANGING

1. Follow **Quilting**, page 86, to mark, layer, and quilt as desired. Our wall hanging was machine quilted in the ditch around borders and hand quilted around letters. To mark outer borders, trace pattern, page 28, and cut out. With straight edge of pattern along eyelet and beginning at a corner, use a fabric-marking pencil to draw around pattern. Use 3 strands of white embroidery floss and a Running Stitch to stitch scalloped design around outer borders.
2. Follow **Making Straight Grain Binding**, page 91, to make 2⁷/₈ yds of 2¹/₂"w binding.
3. Follow **Making a Hanging Sleeve**, page 89, to make and attach a hanging sleeve to wall hanging.
4. Follow **Attaching Binding with Mitered Corners**, page 91, to attach binding to quilt.

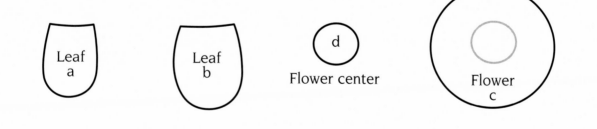

Leaf a

Leaf b

d

Flower center

Flower c

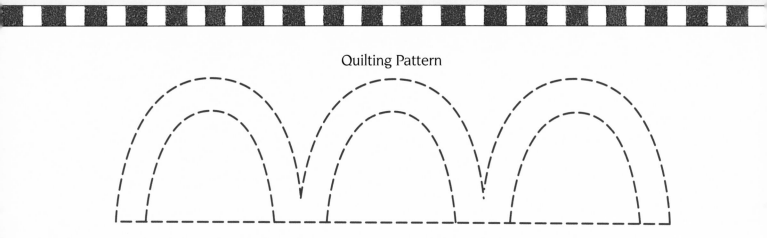

Quilting Pattern

Continued on page 30.

Basket Liner

YARDAGE REQUIREMENTS

Yardage is based on 45" (114 cm) wide fabric.

Rectangular basket
Pink print fabric
Scraps of dark pink print, green print, and
  yellow solid fabrics for flowers and leaves

You will also need:

Bright pink medium rickrack
One 1⅛" (29 mm) diameter button from
  covered button kit
Freezer paper
Plush felt
Fabric glue

MAKING THE BASKET LINER

Use ½" seam allowance for all seams.

1. To determine size of basket liner bottom, measure the width and length of the top edge of your basket. Add 1" to both dimensions and cut pink print fabric to these measurements.

2. Measure the height of basket and add 5". Cut 2 side strips to determined measurement x the width of liner bottom and 2 side strips to determined measurement x the length of liner bottom.

3. Matching right sides, sew sides to liner bottom, then sew sides together to make corners.

4. For hem, turn top edge of liner ¼" to wrong side and press. Turn 1" to wrong side and hem. Measure around top edge of liner and cut a piece of bright pink rickrack this measurement plus 2". Beginning at center back, sew rickrack around right side of liner 1" from top edge.

5. Using pattern, trace flower onto dull side of freezer paper. Iron freezer paper, shiny side down, onto wrong side of fabric piece. Matching right sides and raw edges, place a second fabric piece underneath. Sew around flower pattern; remove freezer paper and trim seam allowances. Cut a slit on one side of flower and turn right side out. Cut a piece of plush felt slightly smaller than flower pattern. Turn flower right side out and insert plush felt; whipstitch slit closed. Follow manufacturer's instructions to cover button with yellow fabric. Sew button to center of flower, going through both layers of flower. Make 3 leaves in the same manner, but leave flat end open for turning. Turn and sew short seam on each leaf for center vein.

6. Refer to photo, page 11, to glue flower and leaves to front of basket liner.

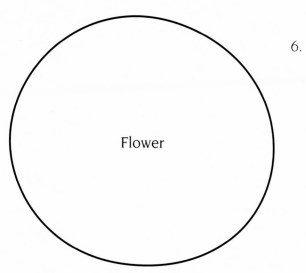

Flower

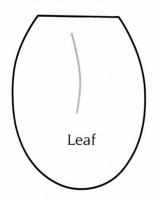

Leaf

Vanity Table

FINISHED SIZE: 42"w x 20"d x 29½"h (107 cm x 51 cm x 75 cm)

YARDAGE REQUIREMENTS

Yardage is based on 45" (114 cm) wide fabric.

3 yds (2.7 m) of yellow print fabric

¾ yd (69 cm) of medium pink print fabric for vanity top

4 yds (3.7 m) of dark pink print fabric for border and lining

½ yd (46 cm) of green print fabric for border

You will also need:

42"w x 20"d x 30"h (107 cm x 51 cm x 76 cm) decorator vanity table kit

3 yds (2.7 m) of dark pink ½" (13 mm) diameter ball fringe

6 yds (5.5 m) of 1¼" (32 mm) wide shirring tape

7" (18 cm) diameter salad plate

#10 carpet tacks

Spray adhesive

Hot glue gun and glue sticks

MAKING THE VANITY TABLE

Use a ½" seam allowance for all seams unless otherwise indicated.

1. Spray top and sides of tabletop with adhesive. Spread medium pink print fabric over tabletop with right side up; cut fabric even with bottom edge of tabletop.

2. For table skirt, cut two 21⅛" x 3 yd strips from yellow print fabric. Sew short ends together to make a 6 yd strip. Cut six 2½" x 42" strips from green print border fabric. Sew short ends together and trim to make a 6 yd strip. Cut six 9" x 2 yd border strips from dark pink print fabric. Sew short ends of 3 border strips together and short ends of 3 lining strips together to make two 6 yd strips.

3. For scallops, draw a line ½" from one long edge on wrong side of lining. Draw a second line 2¾" from first line. Beginning in center and working toward each short end, align edge of plate with first drawn line and short edge of lining; draw around plate on lining between drawn lines. Continue drawing scallops along lining. Press top (unmarked edge) of lining ½" to wrong side.

4. For skirt, matching long edges, sew green print border, then dark pink print border to yellow print fabric piece; press seam allowances toward borders.

5. Matching right sides and long edges, sew lining and border pieces together along scallop lines. Cut away excess fabric below scallops, leaving a ¼" seam allowance. Sew along short ends. Clip curves and corners. Turn border right side out; press. Sew lining to skirt.

6. Press top edge of skirt ⅝" to wrong side. Follow manufacturer's instructions to sew shirring tape to wrong side of skirt along top edge.

7. Follow manufacturer's instructions to assemble table.

8. With top edge of skirt even with top edge of table, tack skirt to center front of table. (**Note:** Drill pilot holes in center of tabletop edge before nailing to avoid cracks or breaks in tabletop.) Nail skirt ends to back of tabletop. Pull gathering strings to gather fabric to table. Tack skirt to table at 3" intervals. Glue gathers between tacks to secure.

9. Beginning and ending at back of table and trimming fringe to fit, glue fringe to table over tacks.

Vanity Seat

FINISHED SIZE: 16½" diameter x 18"h (42 cm x 46 cm)

YARDAGE REQUIREMENTS

Yardage is based on 45" (114 cm) wide fabric.

   1 yd (91 cm) of pink print fabric for seat
   1⅜ yds (1.3 m) of green print fabric for ruffle
   2⅛ yds (1.9 m) of yellow print fabric for skirt
   Scrap of yellow solid fabric for button cover
   1 yd (91 cm) of batting

You will also need:

   16½" diameter x 18"h (42 cm x 46 cm)
      decorator stool kit
   18" x 18" (46 cm x 46 cm) square of 2" (5 cm)
      thick foam
   1½" (3.8 cm) diameter button from covered
      button kit
   1⅝ yds (1.5 m) of dark pink ½" (13 mm)
      diameter ball fringe
   Craft glue
   Fabric glue

MAKING THE VANITY SEAT

Use a ½" seam allowance for all seams.

1. Drill 2 small holes 1" apart through center of stool seat.
2. Cut foam same size as stool seat; glue to seat 1" from edges. With foam on top of stool seat, cover seat with batting and pink print fabric; smooth to bottom of seat. Staple batting and fabric to bottom of seat.
3. Follow manufacturer's instructions to cover button with yellow fabric. Thread needle with 2 to 3 lengths of heavy-duty thread. Passing needle through holes in seat, stitch button to seat. Knot thread ends at bottom of seat to secure.

4. Cut two 21" x 72" pieces from yellow print fabric for skirt. Sew short ends together to make a tube. For hem, press one raw edge ¾" to wrong side twice; topstitch to secure.
5. Cut five 8" x 45" strips from green print fabric for ruffle. Sew short ends together to make a tube. Matching wrong sides and raw edges, press tube in half. Baste ¼" from raw edges. Place tube for ruffle over tube for skirt. Gather ruffle to fit skirt. Matching raw edges, sew ruffle to skirt.
6. To gather skirt, baste around skirt ½" from top edge. Pull thread ends to gather skirt to fit seat. Concealing seams under seat, staple top of skirt to bottom of seat.
7. Glue dark pink ball fringe around edge of seat.
8. Follow manufacturer's instructions to assemble stool.

Princess Pillowcase & Sheet

YARDAGE REQUIREMENTS

Yardage is based on 45" (114 cm) wide fabric.

¼ yd (23 cm) **each** of light pink and green print fabrics

⅛ yd (11 cm) **each** of dark pink and yellow print fabrics

Scrap of yellow solid fabric for crown

You will also need:

Paper-backed fusible web

Stabilizer

Fusible interfacing

Canary medium rickrack

Twin size ivory sheet and standard pillowcase

CUTTING OUT THE PIECES

*Follow **Rotary Cutting**, page 83, and **Preparing Fusible Appliqué Pieces**, page 85, to cut fabric. All measurements include a ¼" seam allowance. Measurements for background rectangle include an extra 2". Trim to correct size after appliquéing. Appliqué patterns, pages 29-30 and 35, do not include seam allowances and are reversed.*

From light pink print fabric:

• Cut 1 background rectangle (**A**) 19½" x 6½".

From dark pink print fabric for appliqués:

• Use patterns to cut letters for "PRINCESS."

• Use patterns to cut 2 diamonds (**a**) and 1 diamond; 1 diamond in reverse (**b**).

From green print fabric:

• Cut 2 inner side borders (**B**) ¾" x 4½".

• Cut 2 inner top/bottom borders (**C**) ¾" x 18".

• Cut 1 strip (**D**) 1½" wide for pillowcase.

• Cut 1 strip (**E**) 1½" wide (piecing as necessary) for sheet.

From yellow print fabric:

• Cut 2 outer side borders (**F**) 1½" x 5".

• Cut 2 outer top/bottom borders (**G**) 1½" x 20".

From yellow solid fabric for appliqué:

• Use pattern to cut 1 crown (**c**).

From fusible interfacing:

• Cut 1 rectangle (**H**) 20" x 7".

MAKING THE PILLOWCASE AND SHEET

Refer to photo, page 15, for placement. Use a ¼" seam allowance for all seams.

1. Position the word, "PRINCESS," on light pink print rectangle (**A**). Fuse, then appliqué in place using matching thread and Satin Stitch. Trim rectangle to measure 17½" x 4½".

2. Sew 2 inner side borders (**B**), then 2 inner top/bottom borders (**C**) to appliquéd block.

3. Sew 2 outer side borders (**F**), then 2 outer top/bottom borders (**G**) to pieced block.

4. Matching right side of pieced block and fusible side of interfacing rectangle, sew block and interfacing together around all edges. Cut a small slit in the center of interfacing and turn block right side out, finger pressing edges.

5. Open top and bottom seams of pillowcase. Position block on pillowcase front with top of block approximately 7" from top edge. Fuse block in place and topstitch around all edges.

6. Position crown (**c**) and diamonds (**a** and **b**) on block; fuse, then appliqué in place using Satin Stitch and gold thread for crown and matching thread for diamonds.

7. For pillowcase trim, measure length of pillowcase hem and cut strip (**D**) determined measurement plus 1". Turn under ¼" on each long edge of strip; press. Pin, then baste yellow rickrack along each long edge of strip. Position trim strip in the center of pillowcase hem and topstitch in place. With right sides together, sew pillowcase seams closed. Turn pillowcase right side out.

8. For sheet trim, measure length of sheet hem and cut strip (**E**) determined measurement plus 1". Turn under ¼" twice on each short edge of strip; topstitch close to short edge. Pin, then baste yellow rickrack along each long edge of strip. Position trim strip in the center of sheet hem and topstitch in place.

Springtime
SUN PORCH

No matter what the weather, heartwarming bouquets of appliquéd flowers will turn your sun porch into a breath of spring! So cuddle up with plump pillows and a comfy quilt while resting your feet on a radiant stool. Complete the mood with a darling wall hanging and a delightful little lamp. Now all you need is a cup of tea!

The perfect complement to a **TULIP BASKET QUILT**, the **TULIP BASKET PILLOW** is a cozy addition to your favorite chair.

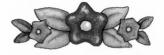

With its painted base and perky appliqués, this captivating **TULIP LAMP** is guaranteed to lighten up any room.

A heartwarming appliqué takes center stage on this unforgettable **TULIP PILLOW**.

Playful pom-pom fringe adds a bit of whimsy to the corresponding **TULIP FOOTSTOOL**.

40

Don't forget the grand finale! With its trio of lovely tulip blocks, a **SPRINGTIME WALL HANGING** is the crowning touch for this garden party.

"People from a planet without flowers would think we must be mad with joy the whole time to have such things about us."

-Iris Murdoch

Tulip Basket Quilt

FINISHED BASKET BLOCK SIZE: 9" x 10" (23 cm x 25 cm)

FINISHED HEART BLOCK SIZE: 9" x 7" (23 cm x 18 cm)

FINISHED QUILT SIZE: 53" x 68" (135 cm x 173 cm)

YARDAGE REQUIREMENTS

Yardage is based on 45" (114 cm) wide fabric.

2³/₈ yds (2.2 m) of green floral print fabric for block backgrounds

1³/₄ yds (1.6 m) of yellow dot fabric for baskets and middle border

³/₈ yd (34 cm) **each** of yellow check, yellow stripe, and yellow floral print fabrics for baskets

Scraps of light green print fabric for tulip stems and light blue and blue print fabrics for tulips

2¹/₈ yds (1.9 m) of medium blue floral print fabric for tulips, ribbon, and outer border

1⁵/₈ yds (1.5 m) of red print fabric for inner border and hearts

18" x 22" (46 cm x 56 cm) piece **each** of red heart print and red check fabrics for hearts

¹/₂ yd (46 cm) of fabric for binding

4¹/₄ yds (3.9 m) of fabric for backing

61" x 76" (1.5 m x 1.9 m) batting

You will also need:

Paper-backed fusible web

Stabilizer

CUTTING OUT THE BLOCKS AND BORDERS

*Follow **Rotary Cutting**, page 83, to cut fabric. All measurements include a ¹/₄" seam allowance. Cutting lengths given for borders are exact. You may wish to add an extra 2" of length at each end for "insurance," trimming borders to fit quilt top center. Measurements for background rectangles include an extra 2". Trim to correct size after appliquéing.*

From green floral print fabric:
- Cut 4 strips 3" wide. From these strips, cut 24 rectangles (A) 3" x 6" for areas 1 and 4 of paper piecing patterns.
- Cut 4 strips 7¹/₂" wide. From these strips, cut 12 background rectangles (B) 11¹/₂" x 7¹/₂" for flower blocks.

- Cut 6 strips 5³/₈" wide. From these strips, cut 24 rectangles (C) 5³/₈" x 9¹/₂" for heart block.

From red print fabric:
- Cut 2 lengthwise inner side borders (D) 2" x 51¹/₂".
- Cut 2 lengthwise inner top/bottom borders (E) 2" x 39¹/₂".

From yellow dot print fabric:
- Cut 2 lengthwise middle side borders (F) 5" x 54¹/₂".
- Cut 2 lengthwise middle top/bottom borders (G) 5" x 48¹/₂".

From remaining width:
- Cut 1 strip 10" wide. From this strip, cut 3 rectangles (H) 10" x 6" for area 3 of basket.
- Cut 1 strip 2³/₄" wide. From this strip, cut 6 squares (I) 2³/₄" x 2³/₄" for areas 2 and 5 of basket.

From *each* yellow check, yellow stripe, and yellow floral print fabric:
- Cut 1 strip 6" wide. From this strip, cut 3 rectangles (H) 10" x 6" for area 3 of basket.
- Cut 1 strip 2³/₄" wide. From this strip, cut 6 squares (I) 2³/₄" x 2³/₄" for areas 2 and 5 of basket.

From *each* yellow dot, yellow check, yellow stripe, and yellow floral print fabrics:
- Cut 3 bias strips (J) 1¹/₂" x 15¹/₂" for basket handles.

From medium blue floral print fabric:
- Cut 2 lengthwise outer side borders (K) 2¹/₂" x 63¹/₂".
- Cut 2 lengthwise outer top/bottom borders (L) 2¹/₂" x 52¹/₂".

From remaining width:
- Cut 4 strips 1³/₄" wide. From these strips, cut 12 rectangles (M) 1³/₄" x 9¹/₂".

From binding fabric:
- Cut 7 strips 2¹/₂" wide.

CUTTING OUT THE APPLIQUÉS

Appliqué patterns, page 53, do not include seam allowances. Follow **Preparing Fusible Appliqué Pieces,** *page 85, to cut out appliqués.*

From light green print fabric:
- Cut 36 stems (a) $^1/_4$" x $1^3/_4$".

From *each* light blue, blue, and medium blue print fabrics:
- Cut 12 tulips (b).

From *each* red heart, red check, and red print fabrics:
- Cut 4 hearts (c).

MAKING THE BLOCKS

Follow **Piecing** *and* **Pressing,** *page 84, and* **Machine Appliqué,** *page 85, to make blocks. Use $^1/_4$" seam allowance for all seams. Refer to* **Block Diagrams,** *page 44, and photo, page 38, for placement.*

Block A

Note: *Use the same yellow print fabric for all basket pieces in each Block A.*

1. Matching wrong sides and long edges, press yellow bias strip (J) in half. Position ends of bias strip, with raw edges facing out, $1^3/_4$" from outer edges of green floral print background rectangle (B). Pin in place. Machine stitch $^1/_4$" from raw edges (**Fig. 1**).

Fig. 1

2. Press strip up and topstitch close to edges (**Fig. 2**).

Fig. 2

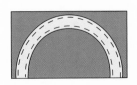

3. Position 3 stems (**a**) and 3 tulips (**b**) (1 of each blue print) on background rectangle. Fuse, then appliqué in place using matching thread and a Satin Stitch to make **Unit 1**. Centering design, trim **Unit 1** to measure $9^1/_2$" x $5^1/_2$". Make 12 **Unit 1**'s.

Unit 1
(make 12)

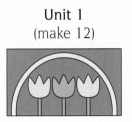

4. To paper piece the basket bottom, make 12 photocopies of each Pattern A and B, page 46. On the wrong side of foundation pattern A, completely cover area 1 with a green print rectangle (**A**). (The right side of the fabric will be facing up.) Pin fabric in place (**Fig. 3**). Fold foundation on line between area 1 and area 2. Trim fabric $^1/_4$" from fold (**Fig. 4**). Unfold foundation.

Fig. 3

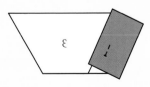

Fig. 4

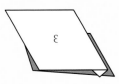

5.   Matching trimmed edges, place yellow print square (**I**) on print rectangle (**A**), right sides together, making sure fabric extends beyond outer edges of area 2. Turn foundation over to front and pin. Sew along line between areas 1 and 2, extending sewing a few stitches beyond beginning and end of line (**Fig. 5**).

Fig. 5

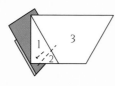

6.   Open out rectangle; press. Pin pieces to foundation (**Fig. 6**).

Fig. 6

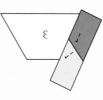

7.   Add yellow basket piece (**H**) in same manner to cover foundation. Trim fabric and foundation ¹/₄" outside edges of pattern.
8.   Repeat Steps 5-6 for pattern B. Trim fabric and foundation ¹/₄" outside edges of pattern.
9.   Matching raw edges and dots, sew pieced foundations A and B together at blue seam to make **Unit 2**. Remove paper foundations. Make 12 **Unit 2**'s.

Unit 2
(make 12)

10. Sew **Unit 1's** and **Unit 2's** of like yellow prints together to make **Block A**. Make 12 **Block A's**.

Block A Diagram
(make 12)

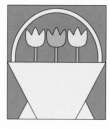

Block B
1.   Matching right sides and long edges, sew 2 green floral rectangles (**C**) and medium blue rectangle (**M**) together as shown to make **Unit 3**. Make 12 **Unit 3's**.

Unit 3
(make 12)

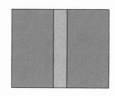

2.   Position red print heart (**c**) on **Unit 3** as shown. Fuse, then appliqué heart in place using matching thread and a Satin Stitch to make **Block B**. Trim block to measure 9¹/₂" x 7¹/₂". Make 12 **Block B's**.

Block B
(make 12)

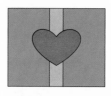

ASSEMBLING THE QUILT TOP
*Refer to **Quilt Top Diagram** to make the quilt top.*
1. Alternating blocks, sew 3 **Block A's** and 3 **Block B's** together as shown to make a vertical row. Make 4 rows.
2. Sew rows together as shown to make **Quilt Top Center**.

ADDING THE BORDERS
Match centers and corners and ease in fullness on all borders.
1. Sew inner side borders (**D**), then inner top/bottom borders (**E**) to **Quilt Top Center**.
2. Sew middle side borders (**F**), then middle top/bottom borders (**G**) to pieced center.
3. Sew outer side borders (**K**), then outer top/bottom borders (**L**) to pieced center to make quilt top.

COMPLETING THE QUILT
1. Follow **Quilting**, page 86, to mark, layer, and quilt as desired. Our quilt was machine quilted.
2. Follow **Making Straight Grain Binding**, page 91, to make 7^1/$_8$ yds of 2^1/$_2$"w binding.
3. Follow **Attaching Binding with Mitered Corners**, page 91, to attach binding to quilt.

Quilt Top Diagram

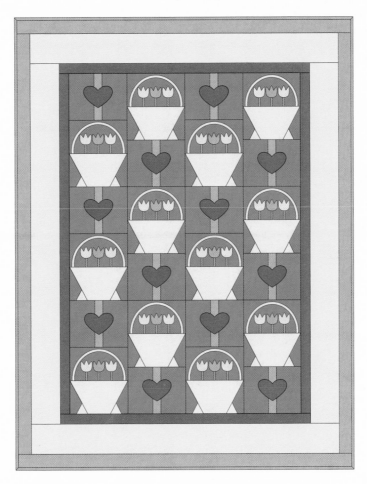

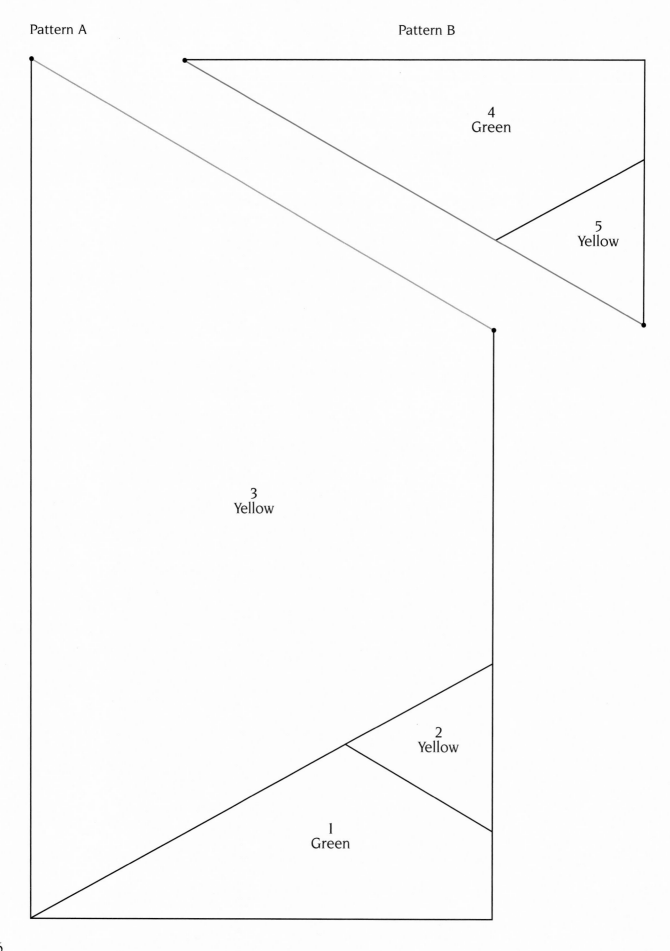

Pattern A

Pattern B

4
Green

5
Yellow

3
Yellow

2
Yellow

1
Green

Tulip Basket Pillow

FINISHED SIZE: 16" x 16" (41 cm x 41 cm)

YARDAGE REQUIREMENTS

Yardage is based on 45" (114 cm) wide fabric.

18" x 22" (46 cm x 56 cm) piece **each** of green floral print fabric for background, yellow dot print fabric for basket, and red print fabric for corner blocks

Scraps of 3 blue print fabrics for tulips and light green print fabric for tulip stems

$^1/_2$ yd (46 cm) of yellow floral print fabric for borders and backing

You will also need:

Paper-backed fusible web

Stabilizer

16" x 16" (41 cm x 41 cm) square pillow form

CUTTING OUT THE PIECES

Follow Rotary Cutting, page 83, to cut fabric. All measurements include a $^1/_4$" seam allowance. Measurements for background rectangle include an extra 2". Trim to correct size after appliquéing.

From green floral print fabric:

- Cut 2 rectangles (**A**) 3" x 6" for areas 1 and 4 of paper piecing patterns.
- Cut 1 background rectangle (**B**) $11^1/_2$" x $7^1/_2$" for flower block.

From yellow dot print fabric:

- Cut 1 rectangle (**C**) 10" x 6" for area 3 of basket.
- Cut 2 squares (**D**) $2^3/_4$" x $2^3/_4$" for areas 2 and 5 of basket.
- Cut 1 bias strip (**E**) $1^1/_2$" x $15^1/_2$" for basket handle.

From yellow floral print fabric:

- Cut 2 side borders (**F**) 4" x $10^1/_2$".
- Cut 2 top/bottom borders (**G**) $9^1/_2$" x $3^1/_2$".
- Cut 2 backing rectangles (**H**) 11" x $16^1/_2$".

From red print fabric:

- Cut 1 strip $3^1/_2$" wide. From this strip, cut 4 rectangles (**I**) 4" x $3^1/_2$".

CUTTING OUT THE APPLIQUES

Follow Preparing Fusible Appliqué Pieces, page 85, to cut appliqués. Appliqué patterns, page 53, do not include seam allowances.

From light green print fabric:

- Cut 3 stems (**a**) $^1/_4$" x $1^3/_4$".

From *each* of 3 blue print fabrics:

- Cut 1 tulip (**b**).

MAKING THE PILLOW

Follow Piecing and Pressing, page 84, and Machine Appliqué, page 85, to make the pillow. Use a $^1/_4$" seam allowance for all seams.

1. Refer to Tulip Basket Quilt, Making the Blocks, Block A, page 43, to make the Basket Block using Paper Piecing Patterns A and B, page 46, and pieces **A-E** and **a-b**.

2. Sew yellow print side borders (**F**) to sides of Basket Block.

3. Sew a red print rectangle (**I**) to each end of yellow print top/bottom borders (**G**). Sew borders to top and bottom of Basket Block to make pillow front.

4. Sew a $^1/_4$" hem (turned under twice) on one long edge of each yellow print backing rectangle (**H**). Matching right sides and raw edges, place pillow backs on pillow front, overlapping finished edges of backs at center. Sew pillow front and backs together. Turn pillow right side out and insert pillow form.

Basket Pillow Diagram

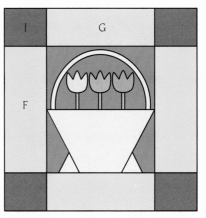

Tulip Pillow

FINISHED SIZE: 16" x 16" (41 cm x 41 cm)

YARDAGE REQUIREMENTS

Yardage is based on 45" (114 cm) wide fabric.

18" x 22" (46 cm x 56 cm) piece **each** of yellow dot print background fabric and medium blue print fabric for tulip and corner blocks

Scraps of 2 blue print fabrics for tulips, light green print fabric for tulip stems and leaves, and red print fabric for heart

$^5/_8$ yd (57 cm) of green floral print fabric for borders and backing

You will also need:

Paper-backed fusible web

Stabilizer

16" x 16" (41 cm x 41 cm) square pillow form

CUTTING OUT THE PIECES

*Follow **Rotary Cutting**, page 83, to cut fabric. All measurements include a $^1/_4$" seam allowance. Measurements for background rectangle include an extra 2". Trim to correct size after appliquéing.*

From yellow dot print fabric:

- Cut 1 background rectangle (**A**) $11^1/_2$" x $12^1/_2$" for heart block.

From medium blue print fabric:

- Cut 1 strip $3^1/_2$" wide. From this strip, cut 4 corner rectangles (**B**) 4" x $3^1/_2$".

From green floral print fabric:

- Cut 2 side borders (**C**) 4" x $10^1/_2$".
- Cut 2 top/bottom borders (**D**) $9^1/_2$" x $3^1/_2$".
- Cut 2 backing rectangles (**E**) 11" x $16^1/_2$".

CUTTING OUT THE APPLIQUÉS

*Follow **Preparing Fusible Appliqué Pieces**, page 85, to cut appliqués. Appliqué patterns, page 53, do not include seam allowances and are reversed.*

From light green print fabric:

- Use pattern to cut 1 stem; cut 1 in reverse (**d**).
- Cut 1 stem (**e**) $^1/_4$" x $4^1/_4$".
- Use pattern to cut 1 leaf; cut 1 in reverse (**f**).

From *each* of 3 blue print fabrics:

- Use pattern to cut 1 tulip (**b**).

From red print fabric:

- Use pattern to cut 1 heart (**g**).

MAKING THE PILLOW

*Follow **Piecing** and **Pressing**, page 84, to make the pillow. Use a $^1/_4$" seam allowance for all seams. Refer to photo, page 40, for placement.*

1. Position stems (**d** and **e**), leaves (**f**), tulips (**b**), and heart (**g**) on yellow dot print rectangle (**A**). Fuse, then appliqué pieces in place using matching thread and a Satin Stitch to make Heart Block. Trim Heart Block to measure $9^1/_2$" x $10^1/_2$".

2. Sew green floral print side borders (**C**) to sides of Heart Block.

3. Sew a medium blue print rectangle (**B**) to each end of green floral print top/bottom borders (**D**). Sew borders to top and bottom of Heart Block to make pillow front.

4. Sew a $^1/_4$" hem (turned under twice) on one long edge of each green floral print backing rectangle (**E**). Matching right sides and raw edges, place pillow backs on pillow front, overlapping finished edges of backs at center. Sew pillow front and backs together. Turn pillow right side out and insert pillow form.

Heart Pillow Diagram

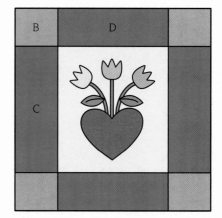

Tulip Lamp

YARDAGE REQUIREMENTS:

Yardage is based on 45" (114 cm) wide fabric.

Wooden desk lamp and shade

³/₈ yd (34 cm) of yellow print fabric

¹/₂ yd (46 cm) of light green print fabric for bias strips

Scraps of assorted fabrics for appliqués

You will also need:

Freezer paper

Spray adhesive

Fabric glue

Double stick fusible web

¹/₂ yd (46 cm) of red medium rickrack

Acrylic paint — white, lavender, green, yellow, and light blue

Clear acrylic sealer

Paintbrush

¹/₄ yd (23cm) of purchased checked double-fold bias binding

CUTTING OUT THE APPLIQUÉS

Follow **Rotary Cutting**, *page 83, and* **Preparing Fusible Appliqué Pieces**, *page 85, to cut fabric. Appliqué patterns, page 53, do not include seam allowances and are reversed.*

From light green print fabric:
- Use pattern to cut 1 stem; cut 1 in reverse (d).
- Cut 1 stem (e) ¹/₄" x 1³/₄".
- Use pattern to cut 1 leaf; cut 1 in reverse (f).

From *each* of 3 blue print fabrics:
- Use pattern to cut 1 tulip (b).

From red print fabric:
- Use pattern to cut 1 heart (c).

MAKING THE LAMP

1. Referring to photo, paint and seal lamp base. Glue piece of checked bias binding around base.
2. Using freezer paper, trace lampshade to make a pattern. Use pattern to cut a piece of yellow print fabric for lampshade. Using spray adhesive, glue fabric to lampshade.

3. Measure around the top of lampshade and cut a piece of red rickrack the determined measurement plus 1". Starting and ending at back, glue rickrack around top of lampshade ³/₄" from top edge.

4. Measure around the top and bottom of lampshade and cut 2 bias strips 2¹/₂" x the determined measurement plus 2" (pieced if necessary). Matching wrong sides and raw edges, press bias strips in half lengthwise. Open out strips and press long edges ¹/₄" to wrong side. Starting and ending at back, glue bias strips around top and bottom edges of lampshade.

5. Referring to photo for placement, position appliqués (b-f) on front of lampshade. Follow manufacturer's instructions to fuse appliqués in place.

THANKS—I HAD A SWELL TIME.

Springtime Wall Hanging

FINISHED BLOCK SIZE: 9 " x 10" (23 cm x 25 cm)
FINISHED SIZE: 39" x 19¹/₂" (99 cm x 50 cm)

YARDAGE REQUIREMENTS

Yardage is based on 45" (114 cm) wide fabric.

1 yd (91 cm) of green floral print fabric for background and borders

18" x 22" (46 cm x 56 cm) piece **each** of yellow dot print, yellow floral print, and yellow check fabric

Scraps of blue print and light green print fabrics for tulips, stems, and leaves

¹/₄ yd (23 cm) of medium blue print fabric for sashings

¹/₈ yd (11 cm) of red print fabric for sashing squares and heart

³/₈ yd (34 cm) of binding fabric

1³/₈ yds (1.3 m) of fabric for backing and hanging sleeve

47" x 28" (1.2 m x .7 m) batting

You will also need:

Paper-backed fusible web

Fabric stabilizer

CUTTING OUT THE PIECES

*Follow **Rotary Cutting**, page 83, to cut fabric. All measurements include a ¹/₄" seam allowance. Measurements for background rectangles include an extra 2". Trim to correct size after appliquéing.*

From green floral print fabric:

*   Cut 2 lengthwise side borders (A) 3¹/₂" x 13".
*   Cut 2 lengthwise top/bottom borders (B) 3¹/₂" x 32¹/₂".

From remaining width:

*   Cut 1 strip 3" wide. From this strip, cut 4 rectangles (C) 3" x 6" for areas 1 and 4 of paper piecing patterns.
*   Cut 2 background rectangles (D) 11¹/₂" x 7¹/₂" for Basket Block.
*   Cut 2 side sashing strips (E) 1¹/₄" x 9" for Heart Block.
*   Cut 2 top/bottom sashing strips (F) 1¹/₄" x 9¹/₂" for Heart Block.

From yellow dot print fabric:

*   Cut 1 background rectangle (G) 10" x 11" for Heart Block.

From *each* yellow check and yellow floral print fabric:

*   Cut 1 rectangle (H) 10" x 6" for area 3 of basket.
*   Cut 2 squares (I) 2³/₄" x 2³/₄" for areas 2 and 5 of basket.
*   Cut 1 bias strip (J) 1¹/₂" x 15¹/₂" for basket handle.

From yellow floral print:

*   Cut 1 strip 3¹/₂" wide. From this strip, cut 4 corner squares (K) 3¹/₂" x 3¹/₂".

From medium blue print fabric:

*   Cut 4 sashing strips (L) 1³/₄" x 10¹/₂".
*   Cut 6 sashing strips (M) 1³/₄" x 9¹/₂".

From red print fabric:

*   Cut 1 strip 1³/₄" wide. From this strip, cut 8 squares (N) 1³/₄" x 1³/₄".

From binding fabric:

*   Cut 4 strips 2¹/₂" wide.

CUTTING OUT THE APPLIQUÉS

*Follow **Preparing Fusible Appliqué Pieces**, page 85, to cut appliqués. Appliqué patterns, page 53, do not include seam allowances and are reversed.*

From light green print fabric:

*   Cut 6 stems (a) ¹/₄" x 1³/₄".
*   Cut 1 stem (c) ¹/₄" x 4¹/₄".
*   Use pattern to cut 1 stem; cut 1 in reverse (d).
*   Use pattern to cut 1 leaf; cut 1 in reverse (f).

From *each* of 3 blue print fabrics:

*   Use pattern to cut 3 tulips (b).

From red print fabric:

*   Use pattern to cut 1 heart (g).

MAKING THE BLOCKS

Follow Piecing and Pressing, page 84, and Machine Applique, page 85, to make the blocks. Use a ¹/₄" seam allowance for all seams.

Basket Block

1. Refer to Tulip Basket Quilt, Making the Blocks, Block A, page 43, to make 2 **Basket Blocks** using background pieces (**C** and **D**), basket pieces (**H**, **I**, and **J**), and flower pieces (**a** and **b**).

Heart Block

1. Position 2 stems (**d**), 1 stem (**c**), 2 leaves (**f**), 3 different tulips (**b**), and heart (**g**) on yellow dot background rectangle (**G**) and fuse in place.
2. Appliqué pieces using matching thread and a Satin Stitch to make **Heart Block**.
3. Trim **Heart Block** to measure 8" x 9".
4. Sew green print side sashing strips (**E**), then green print top/bottom sashing strips (**F**) to **Heart Block**.

Heart Block

ASSEMBLING THE WALL HANGING

Refer to Wall Hanging Top Diagram for placement.

1. Sew 4 medium blue sashing strips (**L**), 2 **Basket Blocks**, and 1 **Heart Block** together as shown to make **Unit 1**.

2. Sew 4 red print squares (**N**) and 3 medium blue sashing strips (**M**) together as shown to make **Unit 2**. Make 2 **Unit 2's**.

3. Sew **Unit 1** and 2 **Unit 2's** together to make **Wall Hanging Top Center**.
4. Sew green floral print side borders (**A**) to sides of **Wall Hanging Top Center**.
5. Sew a yellow floral square (**K**) to each end of green floral print top/bottom borders (**B**). Sew borders to top and bottom of **Wall Hanging Top Center** to make **Wall Hanging Top**.

COMPLETING THE WALL HANGING

1. Follow **Quilting**, page 86, to mark, layer, and quilt as desired. Our wall hanging was machine quilted.
2. Follow **Making Straight Grain Binding**, page 91, to make 3⁵/₈ yds of 2¹/₂"w binding.
3. Follow **Making A Hanging Sleeve**, page 89, to make and attach a hanging sleeve to wall hanging.
4. Follow **Attaching Binding with Mitered Corners**, page 91, to attach binding to quilt.

Wall Hanging Top Diagram

Tulip Footstool

FINISHED SIZE: 11" x 11" (28 cm x 28 cm)

YARDAGE REQUIREMENTS

Yardage is based on 45" (114 cm) wide fabric.

> 20" x 20" (51 cm x 51 cm) piece of yellow dot print background fabric
>
> Scraps of assorted blue, light green, and red print fabrics for appliqués

You will also need:

> Paper-backed fusible web
> Fabric stabilizer
> Fabric glue
> 11" x 11" (28 cm x 28 cm) footstool
> Acrylic paint — blue, yellow, white, and lavender
> Clear acrylic sealer
> Paintbrush
> 16" x 16" (41 cm x 41 cm) piece of batting
> 1³/₈ yds (1.3 m) of red medium rickrack
> 1³/₈ yds (1.3 m) of light blue ¹/₂" (13 mm) diameter ball fringe

CUTTING OUT THE APPLIQUÉS

Follow **Rotary Cutting***, page 83, and* **Preparing Fusible Appliqué Pieces***, page 85, to cut fabric. Appliqué patterns, page 53, do not include seam allowances and are reversed.*

From light green print fabric:

- Use pattern to cut 1 stem; cut 1 in reverse (**d**).
- Cut 1 stem (**a**) ¹/₄" x 4¹/₄".
- Use pattern to cut 1 leaf; cut 1 in reverse (**f**).

From *each* of 3 blue print fabrics:

- Use pattern to cut 1 tulip (**b**).

From red print fabric:

- Use pattern to cut 1 heart (**g**).

MAKING THE FOOTSTOOL

Refer to photo, page 40, for placement.

1. Position stems (**a** and **d**), leaves (**f**), tulips (**b**), and heart (**g**) on yellow dot print background square. Fuse, then appliqué pieces in place using matching thread and a Satin Stitch.
2. Paint and seal legs of footstool.
3. Cover footstool with batting, bringing batting over sides and stapling in place on bottom of footstool.
4. Center appliquéd fabric on top of footstool. Bring fabric over sides and pull taut. Staple fabric to bottom of footstool.
5. Glue red rickrack, then light blue ball fringe around edges of footstool.

Cut here for lamp shade

d

c

f

b

g

So-Sweet
SEWING SPACE

Say "sew" long to your dreary crafting area — this charmingly checkered sewing room is functional *and* fun! You'll adore the timeless tote and tailored chair cover. And don't forget to deck the walls with blooming basket liners, a sewing organizer, a beribboned memo board, and a quotable wall hanging. What fun!

You'll find a place for everything in this clever **SEWING ORGANIZER** embellished with "fried egg flower" appliqués.

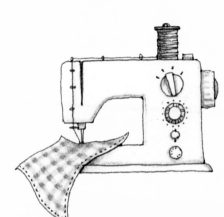

An array of mismatched buttons perks up this **BUTTON BORDER WALL HANGING**, while simple embroidery spells out an inspiring quotation.

Whatever you can do, or dream you can, Begin it.

Embellished with dimensional blossoms, these **SEWING BASKET CUFFS** *look so-smart with their checkerboard backgrounds and red rickrack trim.*

Slip a bit of charm
on your sewing chair
with a tailor-made
CHAIR COVER.

With its handy
drawstring closure, this
SEWING TOTE BAG
is just the thing for
keeping your odds and
ends together.

Polka-dot ribbon and novelty buttons with a "Mary" theme dress up a fabric-covered **MEMO BOARD**.

Sewing Organizer

FINISHED SIZE: 18" x 24" (46 cm x 61 cm)

YARDAGE REQUIREMENTS

Yardage is based on 45" (114 cm) wide fabric.

1¼ yds (1.1 m) of black/white mini check fabric

⅜ yd (34 cm) of red print fabric

Scraps of assorted fabrics for appliqués and stuffed flower and leaves

You will also need:

17" (43 cm) wide hanger

Paper-backed fusible web

Stabilizer

One 1⅛" (29 mm) diameter button from covered button kit

Plush felt

Fabric glue

17½" x 18" (44 cm x 46 cm) piece of cardboard

CUTTING OUT THE PIECES

Follow Rotary Cutting, page 83, and Preparing Fusible Appliqué Pieces, page 85, to cut fabric. All measurements include a ½" seam allowance. Appliqué patterns, page 60, do not include seam allowances and are reversed.

From black and white check fabric:

- Cut 1 front (**A**) 19" x 25".
- Cut 1 pocket (**B**) 19" x 12".
- Cut 1 lower back (**C**) 19" x 18½".
- Cut 1 upper back (**D**) 19" x 10".
- Cut 1 strip (**E**) 1½" x 8½".

From red print fabric:

- Cut 2 pockets (**F**) 19" x 10".

From assorted fabrics for appliqués:

- Use pattern to cut 10 leaves (**a**).
- Use pattern to cut 6 flowers (**b**).
- Use pattern to cut 6 flower centers (**c**).

MAKING THE SEWING ORGANIZER

Follow Piecing and Pressing, page 84, to make the organizer. Use a ½" seam allowance for all seams unless otherwise indicated. Refer to photo, page 55, for placement.

1. Matching wrong sides, fold pocket (**B**) in half lengthwise; press.
2. Position 5 leaves (**a**), 3 flowers (**b**), and 3 flower centers (**c**) on pocket. Fuse, then appliqué pieces in place using matching thread and Satin Stitch.
3. Matching right sides, fold pockets (**F**) in half lengthwise. Sew long edges together. Turn right side out and press.
4. Referring to **Fig. 1** for placement, baste pockets to organizer front (**A**) at side edges.

Fig. 1

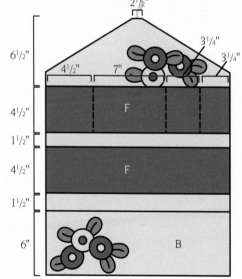

5. Topstitch top and middle pockets to organizer front along bottom edge. Topstitch top pocket at intervals indicated in **Fig. 1**.

6. Press 1 long edge of upper back (**D**) $1/4$" to wrong side; press $1/4$" to wrong side again. Topstitch folded edge in place. Repeat for 1 long edge of lower back (**C**).

7. Matching right sides and raw edges, position upper back on organizer front. Centering hanger horizontally and leaving a $1/2$" seam allowance at top of organizer, place hanger on fabric pieces. Trace outline of hanger on fabric. Cut front and upper back $1/2$" from marked line. Separate front and upper back pieces.

8. Position 5 leaves (**a**), 3 flowers (**b**), and 3 flower centers (**c**) at top right of organizer front. Fuse, then appliqué pieces in place using matching thread and Satin Stitch.

9. Matching trimmed edges and right sides, sew upper back and organizer front together along marked line, leaving a $2^1/2$" opening at center of seam to insert hanger. Trim seam allowances.

10. Matching right sides and raw edges, sew lower back to organizer front. Turn right side out; press. Insert cardboard in lower portion of organizer.

11. For stuffed flower, use patterns, page 31, to trace flower onto dull side of freezer paper. Iron freezer paper, shiny side down, onto wrong side of fabric piece. Matching right sides and raw edges, place a second fabric piece underneath. Sew around flower pattern; remove freezer paper and trim seam allowances. Cut a slit on one side of flower and turn right side out. Cut a piece of plush felt slightly smaller than flower pattern. Insert plush felt; whipstitch slit closed. Make 3 leaves in the same manner, but leave straight end open for turning. Turn, stuff, and sew center vein on each leaf. Follow manufacturer's instructions to cover button with yellow fabric. Sew button to center of flower, going through all layers of flower.

12. Matching right sides and long edges, use $1/4$" seam allowance to sew 1 short and long edge of fabric strip (**E**) together. Turn tube right side out. Cover hanger hook with tube; glue in place at bottom of hook.

13. Glue stuffed flower and leaves to front of organizer at base of hook.

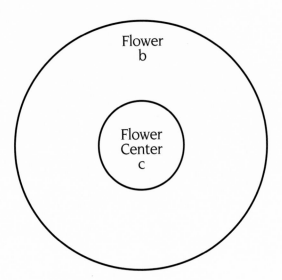

Flower
b

Flower
Center
c

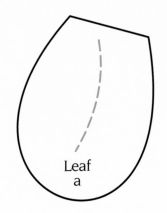

Leaf
a

Button Border Wall Hanging

FINISHED SIZE: 22³/₄" x 17¹/₂" (58 cm x 44 cm)

YARDAGE REQUIREMENTS

Yardage is based on 45" (114 cm) w fabric.

18" x 22" (46 cm x 56 cm) piece of white solid fabric

¹/₂ yd (46 cm) **each** of red print fabric and black/white check (we used ¹/₄") fabric

³/₄ yd (69 cm) of black/white mini check fabric

Scraps of assorted fabrics for appliqués

¹/₂ yd (46 cm) of binding fabric

1 yd (91 cm) of fabric for backing and hanging sleeve

31" x 26" (79 cm x 66 cm) batting

You will also need:

Paper-backed fusible web

Embroidery floss — black and assorted colors

2³/₈ yds (2.2 m) of red jumbo rickrack

Assorted buttons

CUTTING OUT THE PIECES

*Follow **Rotary Cutting**, page 83, to cut fabric. All measurements include a ¹/₄" seam allowance. Measurements for background rectangle include an extra 2". Trim to correct size after appliquéing.*

From white solid fabric:

• Cut 1 background rectangle (A) 16¹/₄" x 11".

From red print fabric:

• Cut 2 lengthwise middle side borders (F) 1" x 10".

• Cut 2 lengthwise middle top/bottom borders (G) 1" x 16¹/₄".

From remaining width:

• Cut 2 side flange strips (B) 1" x 9".

• Cut 2 top/bottom flange strips (C) 1" x 14¹/₄".

From black and white check fabric:

• Cut 2 lengthwise inner side borders (D) 1" x 9".

• Cut 2 lengthwise inner top/bottom borders (E) 1" x 15¹/₄".

From mini check fabric:

• Cut 2 lengthwise outer side borders (H) 3¹/₂" x 11".

• Cut 2 lengthwise outer top/bottom borders (I) 3¹/₂" x 22¹/₄".

CUTTING OUT THE APPLIQUÉS

*Follow **Preparing Fusible Appliqué Pieces**, page 85, to cut appliqués. Appliqué patterns, page 63, do not include seam allowances and are reversed.*

From assorted print fabrics:

• Using patterns, cut 3 leaves (**a**), 2 **each** of leaves (**d**, **e**, and **h**) and 4 of leaf (**i**).

• Using patterns, cut 1 flower (**b**) and 2 each of flowers (**f** and **j**).

• Using patterns, cut 1 **flower center** (**c**) and 2 **each** of flower centers (**g** and **k**).

MAKING THE WALL HANGING TOP

*Follow **Piecing** and **Pressing**, page 84, to make the wall hanging top. Refer to Wall Hanging Diagram, page 62, for placement. Use a ¹/₄" seam allowance for all seams.*

1. Photocopy verse, page 63, at 155%. Center white background rectangle (A) over verse and trace. Use 3 strands of black embroidery floss and a Stem Stitch to stitch verse. Use 3 strands of black embroidery floss to add French Knots.

2. Position leaves, flowers, and flower centers (a-k) on embroidered center. Fuse appliqué pieces in place. Trim center to measure 14¹/₄" x 9".

3. Fold flange strips (**B** and **C**) in half lengthwise with wrong sides together; press. Matching right sides and raw edges and overlapping ends, sew side flange strips, then top/bottom flange strips to **Wall Hanging Top Center**.

4. Sew inner side borders (**D**), then inner top/bottom borders (**E**) to **Wall Hanging Top Center**.

5. Sew middle side borders (**F**), then middle top/bottom borders (**G**) to pieced center.

6. Sew outer side borders (**H**), then outer top/bottom borders (**I**) to pieced center.

7. Sew two 17" lengths of rickrack to outer side edges, then two 22¹/₄" lengths of rickrack to outer top/bottom edges to make **Wall Hanging Top**.

COMPLETING THE WALL HANGING

1. Follow **Quilting**, page 86, to mark, layer, and quilt as desired. Our wall hanging was machine quilted in the ditch around borders.

2. Sew assorted buttons to inner and outer borders using 6 strands of matching embroidery floss.

3. Cut a 16" square of binding fabric. Follow **Making Continuous Bias Strip Binding**, page 90, to make 2⁵/₈ yds of 2¹/₂"w binding.

4. Follow **Making a Hanging Sleeve**, page 89, to make and attach a hanging sleeve to wall hanging.

5. Follow **Attaching Binding with Mitered Corners**, page 91, to attach binding to wall hanging.

Wall Hanging Diagram

62

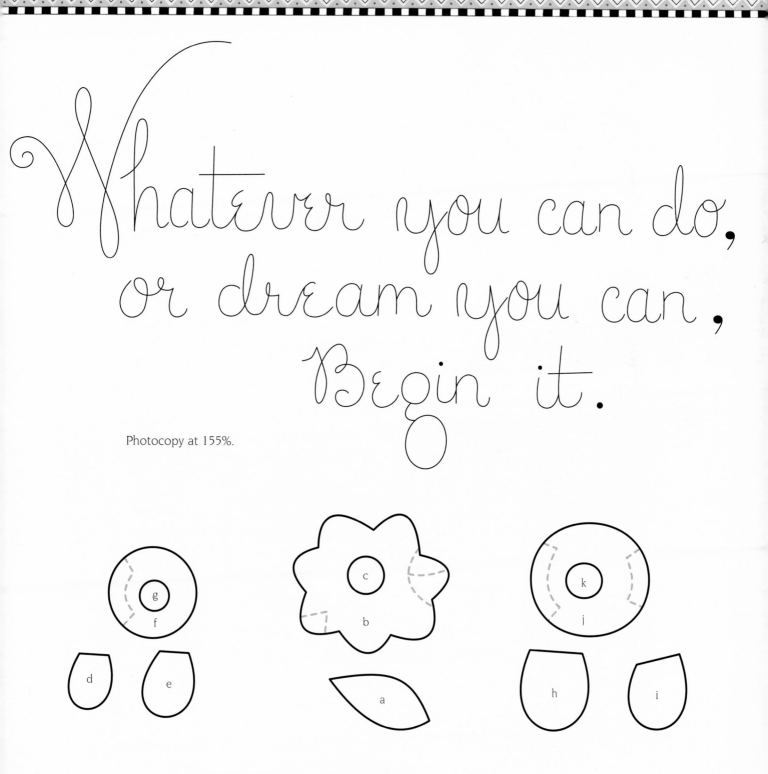

Whatever you can do,
or dream you can,
Begin it.

Photocopy at 155%.

Sewing Basket Cuff

YARDAGE REQUIREMENTS:

Yardage is based on 45" (114 cm) wide fabric.

Basket with handle

Black/white mini check fabric

Scraps of assorted fabrics for stuffed flower
and leaves

You will also need:

Fabric glue

Red jumbo rickrack

Freezer paper

One 1¹/₈" (29 mm) diameter button from
covered button kit

Plush felt

MAKING THE BASKET CUFF

*Refer to photo, page 56, for placement. Use ¹/₂" seam
allowance for all seams.*

1. To determine length of cuff, measure around
the top edge of basket and add 1". To
determine height of cuff, measure height of
basket. Cut a strip of fabric determined height x
determined length. Turn one long edge of fabric
strip ¹/₂" to wrong side and press. On wrong
side of strip, center rickrack over pressed edge
and sew in place. Turn 1 short edge of strip ¹/₂"
to wrong side and press.

2. To determine length of handle slit, measure
width of handle. Approximately 1¹/₄" from
remaining long edge, cut a lengthwise slit the
determined measurement plus 1" (**Fig. 1**).

Fig. 1

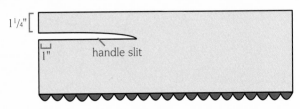

3. Position cuff on basket with 1 end of slit (shown
in red) at edge of handle (**Fig. 2**). Beginning at
handle, glue cuff to inside of basket. Overlap
short edges of cuff and glue in place.

Fig. 2

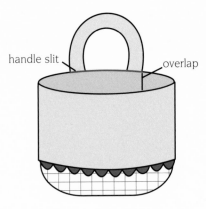

4. For stuffed flower, use patterns, page 31, to
trace flower onto dull side of freezer paper. Iron
freezer paper, shiny side down, onto wrong side
of fabric piece. Matching right sides and raw
edges, place a second fabric piece underneath.
Sew around flower pattern; remove freezer
paper and trim seam allowances. Cut a slit on
one side of flower and turn right side out. Cut a
piece of plush felt slightly smaller than flower
pattern. Turn flower right side out and insert
plush felt; whipstitch slit closed. Make 3 leaves
in the same manner, but leave straight end
open for turning. Turn, stuff, and sew center
vein on each leaf. Follow manufacturer's
instructions to cover button with yellow fabric.
Sew button to center of flower, going through
all layers of flower.

5. Glue flower and leaves to front of basket liner
cuff.

Chair Cover

YOU WILL NEED:

Yardage is based on 45" (114 cm) wide fabric.
- Square-backed upholstered chair
- Assorted fabrics for slipcover
- Scraps of assorted fabrics for appliqués
- Newsprint
- Paper-backed fusible web
- Stabilizer
- Two ⁷/₈" (22 mm) diameter buttons from covered button kit

MAKING THE CHAIR COVER

Cutting the Pieces

Note: To make cutting easier, enter all measurements in table. Refer to Fig. 1 for placement.

1. For **Seat**, measure across front of chair seat (**A**), back of chair seat (**B**), and depth of chair seat (**C**) and add 1" to each measurement. Using these measurements, draw pattern for chair seat on newsprint. Cut out pattern and use to cut one chair seat from fabric.

2. For **Skirt Front**, determine the desired length of skirt and add 1" (**D**). Use this measurement and measurement A to cut **Skirt Front**.

3. For **Skirt Sides**, measure side of chair seat and add 1" (**E**). Use this measurement and measurement D to cut 2 **Skirt Side**s.

4. For **Top**, cut a piece of fabric 12" (measurement **F**) x measurement **B**.

5. For **Middle Back** pieces, cut 2 pieces of fabric 2" (measurement **G**) x measurement **B**.

6. For **Bottom Front** (**H**), measure **Chair Back Front** (**I**) and subtract 4¹/₂". Cut a piece of fabric this measurement x measurement **B**.

7. For **Bottom Back** (**J**), add measurement D and measurement H and subtract 1". Cut a piece of fabric this measurement x measurement **B**.

8. For **Gussets**, measure depth (at deepest area) of chair back and add 1" (**K**). For **Top Gusset** pieces, cut 2 pieces of fabric 5¹/₂" x measurement **K**. For **Middle Gusset** pieces, cut 2 pieces of fabric 2" x measurement **K**. For **Bottom Gusset** pieces, cut 2 pieces of fabric measurement J x measurement K.

Chair Measurement Table

Chair Cover Piece	Measurement	Cutting Measurement
Front Chair Seat (**A**)	____" + 1" =	(____")
Back Chair Seat (**B**)	____" + 1" =	(____")
Chair Seat Depth (**C**)	____" + 1" =	(____")
Skirt Length (**D**)	____" + 1" =	(____")
Chair Seat Side (**E**)	____" + 1" =	(____")
Top (**F**)		(12")
Middle Front and Back (**G**)		(2")
Chair Back Front (**I**)		(____")
Bottom Front (**H**)	I (____") – 4¹/₂" =	(____")
Bottom Back (**J**)	D(___")+H(___")–1"=	(____")
Gusset Depth (**K**)	____" + 1" =	(____")

Fig. 1

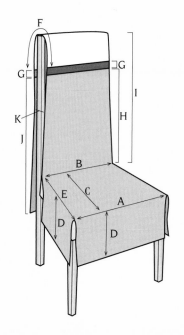

Assembling the Chair Cover

Appliqué patterns are reversed and do not include seam allowances. Match right sides and raw edges and use a 1/2" seam allowance for all seams.

1. Sew **Bottom Back**, **Middle Back**, **Top**, **Middle Front**, and **Bottom Front** pieces together as shown to make **Chair Cover Back**.

Chair Cover Back

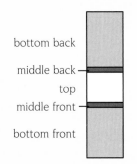

bottom back
middle back
top
middle front
bottom front

2. Follow **Preparing Fusible Appliqué Pieces**, page 85, and use patterns, page 60, to cut 5 leaves (**a**), 2 flowers (**b**), and 2 flower centers (**c**) from assorted fabrics. Referring to photo, position appliqués on back of **Top**. Fuse, then appliqué pieces in place using matching thread and Satin Stitch.

3. Sew **Top**, **Middle**, and **Bottom Gusset** pieces together to make **Gusset**. Make 2 **Gussets**.

Gusset
(make 2)

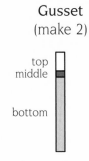

top
middle
bottom

4. Matching bottom edge of **Gusset** and bottom back edge of chair cover, sew each **Gusset** to **Chair Back**, clipping seam allowances at corners.

5. Sew a 1/4" hem (turned under twice) on each short edge of **Skirt Front**.

6. Sew **Chair Back**, **Seat**, and **Skirt Front** together.

7. Sew a 1/4" hem (turned under twice) on 1 short edge of each **Side Skirt**. Sew each **Side Skirt** to **Seat** and **Gusset**.

8. For binding, measure bottom edge of **Chair Cover** and **Skirt Front**. Cut 2 strips of fabric 2 1/2" wide x the determined measurements (pieced as necessary) plus 1". Matching wrong sides and raw edges, press strips in half lengthwise. Open out strips and press long edges 1/4" to wrong side. Turn under short edges of binding 1/4"; press. Sew binding to bottom of **Chair Cover** and **Skirt Front**.

9. For bow, cut a 3" x 36" piece of fabric. Matching right sides and long edges and leaving an opening for turning, sew raw edges together. Turn right side out and blindstitch opening closed. Press. Tie fabric strip in a bow and referring to photo, glue to middle back section of chair cover.

10. For button tabs, follow manufacturer's instructions to cover 2 buttons with fabric. Cut 2 fabric strips 2" x 5". Matching wrong sides and raw edges, press strips in half lengthwise. Open out strips and press long edges 1/4" to wrong side. Sew pressed edges together. Fold strip in half, forming a point as shown in **Fig. 2**. Topstitch point in place close to edge as shown.

Fig. 2

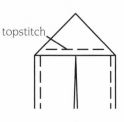

topstitch

11. Place chair cover on chair; determine position for button tabs. Sew tabs to **Skirt Front** and buttons to **Skirt Sides**.

Sewing Tote Bag

FINISHED SIZE: 14½" x 15½" (37 cm x 39 cm)

YARDAGE REQUIREMENTS

Yardage is based on 45" (114 cm) wide fabric.

¼ yd (23 cm) **each** of black/white mini check and large black/white check (we used 1⅛") fabrics

⅛ yd (11 cm) of red floral print fabric

1⅛ yds (1.0 m) of red print fabric

You will also need:

Two 15" x 18½" (38 cm x 47 cm) pieces of batting

Embroidery floss — black

CUTTING OUT THE PIECES

All measurements include a ¼" seam allowance.

From black/white mini check fabric:

- Cut 2 rectangles (**A**) 15" x 6".

From red floral print fabric:

- Cut 2 rectangles (**B**) 15" x 1¼".

From large black/white check fabric:

- Cut 2 rectangles (**C**) 15" x 4¼".

From red print fabric:

- Cut 2 rectangles (**D**) 15" x 7".
- Cut 2 rectangles (**E**) 15" x 18½" for lining.
- Cut 2 rectangles (**F**) 3" x 25½" for straps.
- Cut 2 rectangles (**G**) 3" x 23" for drawstring.

MAKING THE TOTE BAG

*Follow **Piecing** and **Pressing**, page 84, to make the tote. Match right sides and raw edges and use a ¼" seam allowance for all seams.*

1. Matching long edges, sew 1 each of rectangles **A-D** together in alphabetical order to make tote front. Repeat for tote back.
2. Sew tote front and back together along sides and bottom. To form bottom corners, match side seams to bottom seam; sew across each corner 1" from end (**Fig. 1**).

Fig. 1

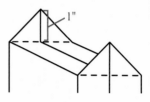

3. Baste each batting piece to wrong side of each lining rectangle (**E**). Follow Step 2 to make lining using lining pieces. Do not turn lining right side out.
4. For straps, fold each rectangle (**F**) in half lengthwise; sew long edges together. Turn straps right side out. Centering seam in back, press. Pin ends of one strap to front of tote 1½" from each side seam. Baste strap in place. Repeat for tote back and remaining strap.
5. With right sides together, place tote inside lining. Sew tote and lining together along top edge, leaving an opening for turning. Turn tote right side out and blindstitch opening closed. Press.
6. To form drawstring casing, topstitch 1" and 2" below top edge of tote. At center of tote, cut an opening between stitching lines, cutting through top layer of fabric only. Using a Blanket Stitch and 3 strands of black embroidery floss, stitch around opening.
7. For drawstring, sew 2 rectangles (**G**) together at 1 short edge. Fold pieced rectangle in half lengthwise. Sew sides and long edges together leaving an opening for turning. Turn drawstring right side out and blindstitch opening closed. Press. Using a safety pin, thread drawstring through casing.

Memo Board

YARDAGE REQUIREMENTS

Yardage is based on 45" (114 cm) wide fabric.

Red print fabric

Black/white check (we used ¹/₄") fabric

You will also need:

Framed bulletin board

³/₈" (9.5 mm) wide grosgrain ribbon

Assorted novelty buttons

Matte finish decoupage medium

Craft glue

Staple gun

Thumbtacks

MAKING THE MEMO BOARD

1. Remove bulletin board from frame and measure the width and length. Add 4" to each measurement. Cut a piece of red print fabric the determined measurements. Cover bulletin board with fabric, using a staple gun to attach fabric to back of board.

2. Referring to photo for placement, attach grosgrain ribbon to bulletin board, stapling ends to back of board.

3. Remove shanks from buttons and glue buttons to thumbtacks. Use thumbtacks to secure ribbons at intersections.

4. Measure the inner and outer length and the width of frame (**Fig. 1**). Cut four strips of black/white check fabric the determined length measurements x the width measurement plus 2", mitering ends of strips as shown in **Fig. 2**.

Fig.1

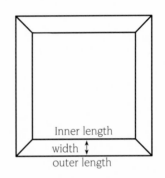

Inner length
width
outer length

Fig.2

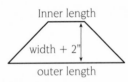

Inner length
width + 2"
outer length

5. Following manufacturer's instructions, apply a coat of decoupage medium to frame. Position fabric strips on frame, overlapping corners and smoothing out air bubbles. Allow fabric to dry. Apply a second coat to seal fabric.

6. Referring to photo, glue grosgrain ribbon over corners of frame.

7. Replace covered bulletin board in frame and secure.

Artful
WALL HANGINGS

Whether you're looking for a homey accent or hoping for something a little more romantic, an engaging wall hanging is just the thing. A cozy cottage with a checkerboard border (page 76) is a welcome addition to any wall, while a clever arrangement of flowers surrounded by a patchwork border is sure to steal your heart.

Use favorite fabric scraps and colored pencil shading to make this **SPRING BOUQUET WALL HANGING** *your own.*

Spring Bouquet Wall Hanging

FINISHED SIZE: 23" x 27" (58 cm x 69 cm)

YARDAGE REQUIREMENTS

Yardage is based on 45" (114 cm) wide fabric.

> 18" x 22" (46 cm x 56 cm) piece of yellow print fabric
>
> Scraps of assorted fabrics for appliqués and outer borders
>
> $^1/_8$ yd (11 cm) of green print fabric
>
> $^1/_4$ yd (23 cm) of binding fabric
>
> 1 yd (91 cm) of fabric for backing and hanging sleeve
>
> 31" x 35" (79 cm x 89 cm) batting

You will also need:

> Paper-backed fusible web
>
> Embroidery floss — green
>
> Colored pencils

CUTTING OUT THE PIECES

Follow **Rotary Cutting**, *page 83, to cut fabric. All measurements include a $^1/_4$" seam allowance.*

From yellow print fabric:

- Cut 1 background rectangle (**A**) $16^1/_2$" x $20^1/_2$".

From green print fabric:

- Cut 2 inner side borders (**B**) $1^1/_2$" x $20^1/_2$".
- Cut 2 inner top/bottom borders (**C**) $1^1/_2$" x $18^1/_2$".

From assorted print fabrics:

- Cut 44 squares (**D**) $2^1/_2$" x $2^1/_2$".

From binding fabric:

- Cut 3 strips $2^1/_2$" wide.

MAKING THE WALL HANGING TOP

Follow **Piecing** *and* **Pressing**, *page 84, to make wall hanging. Use a $^1/_4$" seam allowance for all seams. Appliqué patterns do not include seam allowances and are reversed. Refer to photo, page 69, and* **Wall Hanging Diagram** *for placement.*

1. Follow **Preparing Fusible Appliqué Pieces**, page 85, to cut out appliqués using patterns (**A-LL**), pages 72-75, and assorted fabrics.
2. Position appliqués in alphabetical order on yellow print background rectangle (**A**) and fuse in place to make wall hanging top center.
3. Stitch tendrils using 4 strands of green embroidery floss and a Chain Stitch. Machine stitch veins on leaves. Shade flowers and leaves with colored pencils as desired.
4. Sew 2 inner side borders (**B**), then 2 inner top/bottom borders (**C**) to wall hanging top center.
5. Sew 11 squares (**D**) together in random order to make **Border Unit**. Make 4 **Border Units**.
6. Sew a **Border Unit** to sides, then to top and bottom of pieced center to make **Wall Hanging Top**.
7. Position 4 heart appliqués on **Wall Hanging Top** and fuse in place.

COMPLETING THE WALL HANGING

1. Follow **Quilting**, page 86, to mark, layer, and quilt as desired. Our wall hanging was machine quilted.
2. Follow **Making Straight Grain Binding**, page 91, to make $3^1/_8$ yds of $2^1/_2$"w binding.
3. Follow **Making a Hanging Sleeve**, page 89, to make and attach a hanging sleeve to wall hanging.
4. Follow **Attaching Binding with Mitered Corners**, page 91, to attach binding to quilt.

Wall Hanging Diagram

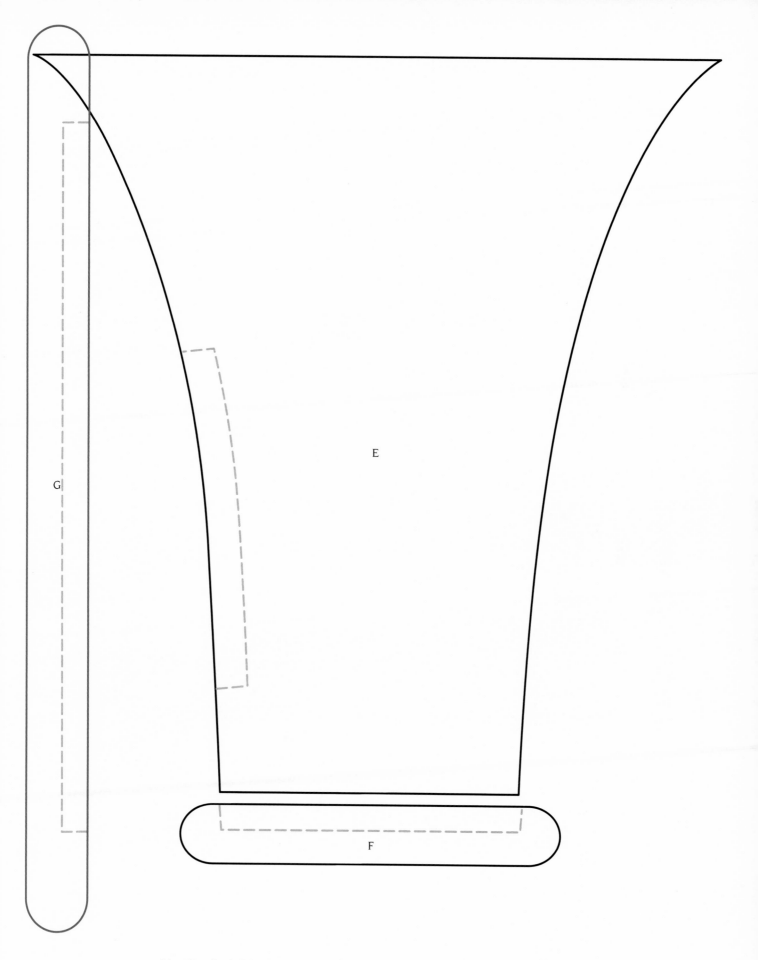

E

G

F

Thanks to time-saving fusible appliqués, this scenic **COTTAGE**

WALL HANGING is easier to make than you might imagine.

Cottage Wall Hanging

FINISHED SIZE: 19¼" x 20¼" (49 cm x 51 cm)

YARDAGE REQUIREMENTS

Yardage is based on 45" (114 cm) wide fabric.

18" x 22" (46 cm x 56 cm) piece of white/blue print background fabric (ours resembled sky)

Scrap of 1⅛" (2.8 cm) black/white check fabric

Scraps of assorted fabrics for appliqués

⅛ yd (11 cm) of blue print fabric for inner border

⅛ yd (11 cm) of ¼" (.6 cm) black/white check fabric for outer border

¼ yd (23 cm) of binding fabric

¾ yd (69 cm) of fabric for backing and hanging sleeve

27" x 28" (69 cm x 71 cm) batting

You will also need:

Paper-backed fusible web

CUTTING OUT THE PIECES

Follow **Rotary Cutting**, *page 83, to cut fabric. All measurements include a ¼" seam allowance.*

From white/blue print fabric:
- Cut 1 background square (A) 13¾" x 13¾".

From 1⅛" black/white check fabric:
- Cut 1 rectangle (B) 1⅝" x 13¾".

From blue print fabric:
- Cut 2 inner side borders (C) 1½" x 14¾".
- Cut 2 inner top/bottom borders (D) 1½" x 15¾".

From ¼" black/white check fabric:
- Cut 2 outer side borders (E) 2" x 16¾".
- Cut 2 outer top/bottom borders (F) 2" x 18¾".

From binding fabric:
- Cut 3 strips 2½" wide.

CUTTING OUT THE APPLIQUÉS

Follow **Preparing Fusible Appliqué Pieces**, *page 85, to cut appliqués. Appliqué patterns, pages 79-82, do not include seam allowances and are reversed.*

From assorted print fabrics:
- Using patterns (**a-z**), cut house, greenery, and fence appliqués.
- Using patterns, cut 5 **each** of leaves (**aa** and **dd**).

- Using pattern, cut 3 leaves (**bb**).
- Using pattern, cut 4 leaves (**cc**).
- Using patterns, cut 2 **each** of flowers (**ee** and **ii**) and 2 **each** of flower centers (**ff** and **jj**).
- Using patterns, cut 6 flowers (**gg**) and 6 flower centers (**hh**).
- Using patterns, cut 1 **each** of flowers (**kk** and **mm**) and 1 **each** of flower centers (**ll** and **nn**).

MAKING THE WALL HANGING TOP

Follow **Piecing** *and* **Pressing**, *page 84, to make the wall hanging. Use ¼" seam allowance for all seams. Refer to photo and* **Wall Hanging Diagram**, *page 78, for placement.*

1. Position house, greenery, and fence appliqués in alphabetical order on white/blue print background square (**A**) and fuse in place to make **Unit 1**.
2. Sew 1⅛" black/white check rectangle (**B**) to bottom of **Unit 1** as shown to make **Wall Hanging Top Center**.
3. Sew 2 inner side borders (**C**), then 2 inner top/bottom borders (**D**) to **Wall Hanging Top Center**.
4. Position flower, flower center, and leaf appliqués in alphabetical order on pieced center and fuse in place.
5. Sew 2 outer side borders (**E**), then 2 outer top/bottom borders (**F**) to pieced center to make **Wall Hanging Top**.

COMPLETING THE WALL HANGING

1. Follow **Quilting**, page 86, to mark, layer, and quilt as desired. Our wall hanging was machine quilted.
2. Follow **Making Straight Grain Binding**, page 91, to make 2½ yds of 2½"w binding.
3. Follow **Making a Hanging Sleeve**, page 89, to make and attach a hanging sleeve to wall hanging.
4. Follow **Attaching Binding with Mitered Corners**, page 91, to attach binding to quilt.

a

b

c

d

e

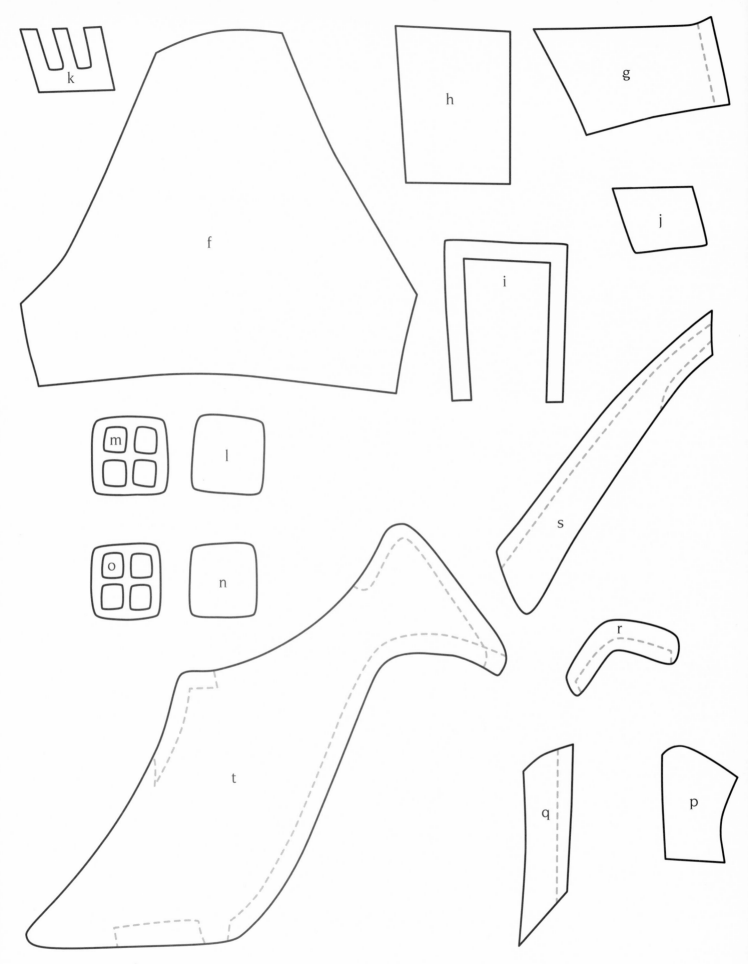

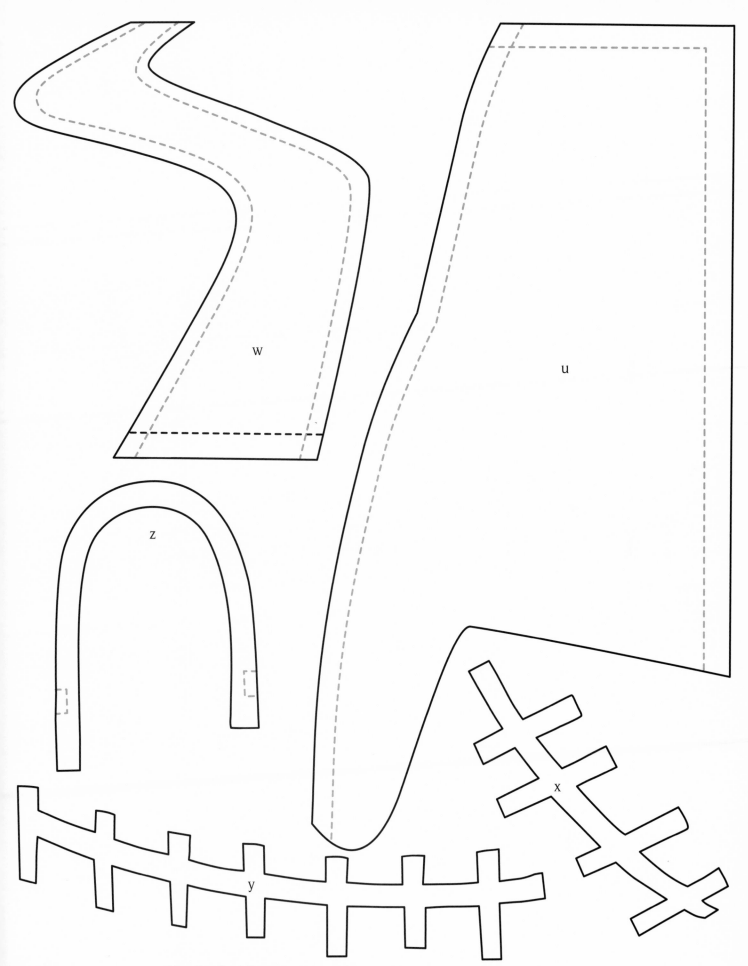

w

u

z

x

y

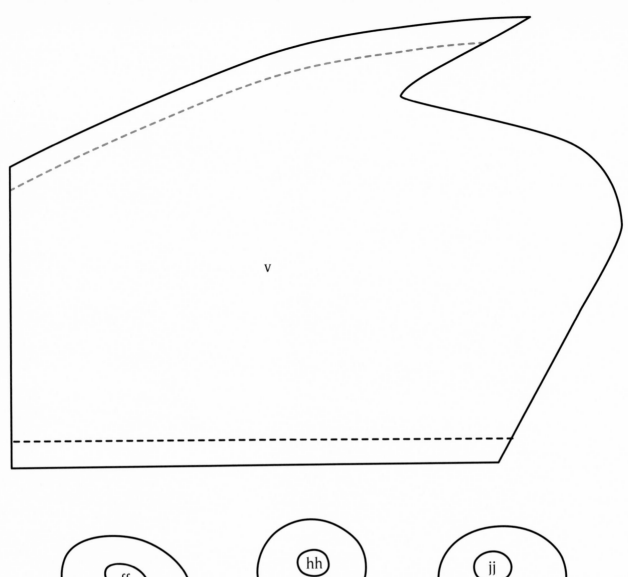

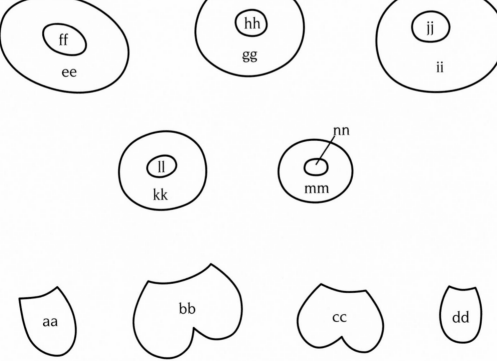

General INSTRUCTIONS

To make your quilting easier and more enjoyable, we encourage you to carefully read all of the general instructions, study the color photographs, and familiarize yourself with the individual project instructions before beginning a project.

FABRICS

SELECTING FABRICS

Choose high-quality, medium-weight 100% cotton fabrics. All-cotton fabrics hold a crease better, fray less, and are easier to quilt than cotton/polyester blends.

Yardage requirements listed for each project are based on 45" wide fabric with a "usable" width of 42" after shrinkage and trimming selvages. Actual usable width will probably vary slightly from fabric to fabric. Our recommended yardage lengths should be adequate for occasional re-squaring of fabric when many cuts are required.

PREPARING FABRICS

We recommend that all fabrics be washed, dried, and pressed before cutting. If fabrics are not pre-washed, washing finished quilt will cause shrinkage and give it a more "antiqued" look and feel. Bright and dark colors, which may run, should always be washed before cutting. After washing and drying fabric, fold lengthwise with wrong sides together and matching selvages.

ROTARY CUTTING

Rotary cutting has brought speed and accuracy to quiltmaking by allowing quilters to easily cut strips of fabric and then cut those strips into smaller pieces.

- Place fabric on work surface with fold closest to you.
- Cut all strips from selvage-to-selvage width of fabric unless otherwise indicated in project instructions.
- Square left edge of fabric using rotary cutter and rulers (**Figs. 1-2**).

Fig. 1

Fig. 2

- To cut each strip required for a project, place ruler over cut edge of fabric, aligning desired marking on ruler with cut edge; make cut (**Fig. 3**).

Fig. 3

- When cutting several strips from a single piece of fabric, it is important to make sure that cuts remain at a perfect right angle to the fold; square fabric as needed.

PIECING

Precise cutting, followed by accurate piecing, will ensure that all pieces of quilt top fit together well.

MACHINE PIECING

- Set sewing machine stitch length for approximately 11 stitches per inch.

- Use neutral-colored general-purpose sewing thread (not quilting thread) in needle and in bobbin.

- An accurate 1/4" seam allowance is essential. Presser feet that are 1/4" wide are available for most sewing machines.

- When piecing, always place pieces right sides together and match raw edges; pin if necessary.

- Chain piecing saves time and will usually result in more accurate piecing.

- Trim away points of seam allowances that extend beyond edges of sewn pieces.

Sewing Strip Sets

When there are several strips to assemble into a strip set, first sew strips together into pairs, then sew pairs together to form strip set. To help avoid distortion, sew seams in opposite directions (**Fig. 4**).

Fig. 4

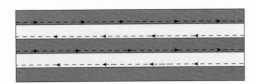

PRESSING

- Use steam iron set on "Cotton" for all pressing.

- Press after sewing each seam.

- Seam allowances are almost always pressed to 1 side, usually toward darker fabric. However, to reduce bulk it may occasionally be necessary to press seam allowances toward the lighter fabric or even to press them open.

- To prevent dark fabric seam allowance from showing through light fabric, trim darker seam allowance slightly narrower than lighter seam allowance.

- To press long seams, such as those in long strip sets, without curving or other distortion, lay strips across width of the ironing board.

MACHINE APPLIQUÉ

Preparing Fusible Appliqué Pieces

White or light-colored fabrics may need to be lined with fusible interfacing before applying fusible web to prevent darker fabrics from showing through.

1. Place paper-backed fusible web, paper side up, over appliqué pattern. Trace pattern onto paper side of web with pencil as many times as indicated in project instructions for a single fabric.
2. Follow manufacturer's instructions to fuse traced patterns to wrong side of fabrics. Do not remove paper backing.
3. Use scissors to cut out appliqué pieces along traced lines. Remove paper backing from all pieces.

Satin Stitch Appliqué

A good satin stitch is a thick, smooth, almost solid line of zigzag stitching that covers the exposed raw edges of appliqué pieces.

1. Pin stabilizer, such as paper or any of the commercially available products, on wrong side of background fabric before stitching appliqués in place.
2. Thread sewing machine with general-purpose thread; use general-purpose thread that matches background fabric in bobbin.
3. Set sewing machine for a medium (approximately $1/8$") zigzag stitch and a short stitch length. Slightly loosening the top tension may yield a smoother stitch.
4. Begin by stitching 2 or 3 stitches in place (drop feed dogs or set stitch length at 0) to anchor thread. Most of the Satin Stitch should be on the appliqué with the right edge of the stitch falling at the outside edge of the appliqué. Stitch over all exposed raw edges of appliqué pieces.

5. (**Note**: Dots on **Figs. 5-10** indicate where to leave needle in fabric when pivoting.) For outside corners, stitch just past corner, stopping with needle in background fabric (**Fig. 5**). Raise presser foot. Pivot project, lower presser foot, and stitch adjacent side (**Fig. 6**).

Fig. 5   Fig. 6

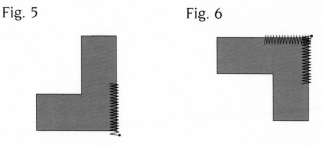

6. For inside corners, stitch just past corner, stopping with needle in appliqué fabric (**Fig. 7**). Raise presser foot. Pivot project, lower presser foot, and stitch adjacent side (**Fig. 8**).

Fig. 7   Fig. 8

7. When stitching outside curves, stop with needle in background fabric. Raise presser foot and pivot project as needed. Lower presser foot and continue stitching, pivoting as often as necessary to follow curve (**Fig. 9**).

Fig. 9

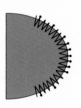

8. When stitching inside curves, stop with needle in appliqué fabric. Raise presser foot and pivot project as needed. Lower presser foot and continue stitching, pivoting as often as necessary to follow curve (**Fig. 10**).

Fig. 10

9. Do not backstitch at end of stitching. Pull threads to wrong side of background fabric; knot thread and trim ends.
10. Carefully tear away stabilizer.

QUILTING

Quilting holds the 3 layers (top, batting, and backing) of the quilt together and can be done by hand or machine. Because marking, layering, and quilting are interrelated and may be done in different orders depending on circumstances, please read entire Quilting section before beginning project.

TYPES OF QUILTING DESIGNS

In the Ditch Quilting
Quilting along seamlines or along edges of appliquéd pieces is called "in the ditch" quilting. This type of quilting should be done on side **opposite** seam allowance and does not have to be marked.

Outline Quilting
Quilting a consistent distance, usually $1/4$", from seam or appliqué is called "outline" quilting. Outline quilting may be marked, or $1/4$" masking tape may be placed along seamlines for quilting guide. (Do not leave tape on quilt longer than necessary, since it may leave an adhesive residue.)

Motif Quilting
Quilting a design, such as a feathered wreath, is called "motif" quilting. This type of quilting should be marked before basting quilt layers together.

Echo Quilting
Quilting that follows the outline of an appliquéd or pieced design with 2 or more parallel lines is called "echo" quilting. This type of quilting does not need to be marked.

Meandering Quilting
Quilting in random curved lines and swirls is called "meandering" quilting. Quilting lines should not cross or touch each other. This type of quilting does not need to be marked.

Stipple Quilting

Meandering quilting that is very closely spaced is called "stipple" quilting. Stippling will flatten the area quilted and is often stitched in background areas to raise appliquéd or pieced designs. This type of quilting does not need to be marked.

MARKING QUILTING LINES

Quilting lines may be marked using fabric marking pencils, chalk markers, water or air soluble pens, or lead pencils.

Simple quilting designs may be marked with chalk or chalk pencil after basting. A small area may be marked, then quilted, before moving to next area to be marked. Intricate designs should be marked before basting using a more durable marker.

Caution: Some marks may be permanently set by pressing. **Test** different markers **on scrap fabric** to find one that marks clearly and can be thoroughly removed.

A wide variety of precut quilting stencils, as well as entire books of quilting patterns, are available. Using a stencil makes it easier to mark intricate or repetitive designs.

To make a stencil from a pattern, center template plastic over pattern and use a permanent marker to trace pattern onto plastic. Use a craft knife with single or double blade to cut channels along traced lines (**Fig. 11**).

Fig. 11

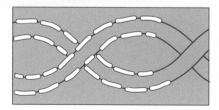

PREPARING THE BACKING

To allow for slight shifting of quilt top during quilting, backing should be approximately 4" larger on all sides. Yardage requirements listed for quilt backings are calculated for 45"w fabric. Using 90"w or 108"w fabric for the backing of a bed-sized quilt may eliminate piecing. To piece a backing using 45"w fabric, use the following instructions.

1. Measure length and width of quilt top; add 8" to each measurement.
2. If determined width is 84" or less, cut backing fabric into 2 lengths slightly longer than determined **length** measurement. Trim selvages. Place lengths with right sides facing and sew long edges together, forming tube (**Fig. 12**). Match seams and press along 1 fold (**Fig. 13**). Cut along pressed fold to form single piece (**Fig. 14**).

Fig. 12   Fig. 13   Fig. 14

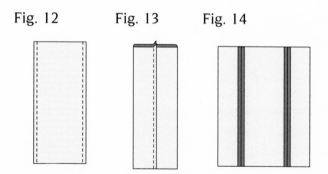

3. If determined width is more than 84", cut backing fabric into 3 lengths slightly longer than determined **width** measurement. Trim selvages. Sew long edges together to form single piece.
4. Trim backing to size determined in Step 1; press seam allowances open.

CHOOSING THE BATTING

The appropriate batting will make quilting easier. For fine hand quilting, choose low-loft batting. All cotton or cotton/polyester blend battings work well for machine quilting because the cotton helps "grip" quilt layers. If quilt is to be tied, a high-loft batting, sometimes called extra-loft or fat batting, may be used to make quilt "fluffy."

Types of batting include cotton, polyester, cotton/polyester blend, wool, cotton/wool blend, and silk.

When selecting batting, refer to package labels for characteristics and care instructions. Cut batting same size as prepared backing.

ASSEMBLING THE QUILT

1. Examine wrong side of quilt top closely; trim any seam allowances and clip any threads that may show through front of the quilt. Press quilt top, being careful not to "set" any marked quilting lines.
2. Place backing **wrong** side up on flat surface. Use masking tape to tape edges of backing to surface. Place batting on top of backing fabric. Smooth batting gently, being careful not to stretch or tear. Center quilt top **right** side up on batting.
3. If hand quilting, begin in center and work toward outer edges to hand baste all layers together. Use long stitches and place basting lines approximately 4" apart (**Fig. 15**). Smooth fullness or wrinkles toward outer edges.

Fig. 15

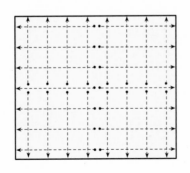

4. If machine quilting, use 1" rustproof safety pins to "pin-baste" all layers together, spacing pins approximately 4" apart. Begin at center and work toward outer edges to secure all layers. If possible, place pins away from areas that will be quilted, although pins may be removed as needed when quilting.

HAND QUILTING

The quilting stitch is a basic running stitch that forms a broken line on quilt top and backing. Stitches on quilt top and backing should be straight and equal in length.

1. Secure center of quilt in hoop or frame. Check quilt top and backing to make sure they are smooth. To help prevent puckers, always begin quilting in the center of quilt and work toward outside edges.
2. Thread needle with 18" - 20" length of quilting thread; knot 1 end. Using thimble, insert needle into quilt top and batting approximately $1/2$" from quilting line. Bring needle up on quilting line (**Fig. 16**); when knot catches on quilt top, give thread a quick, short pull to "pop" knot through fabric into batting (**Fig. 17**).

Fig. 16   Fig. 17

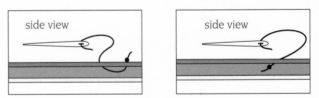

3. Holding needle with sewing hand and placing other hand underneath quilt, use thimble to push tip of needle down through all layers. As soon as needle touches finger underneath, use that finger to push tip of needle only back up through layers to top of quilt. (The amount of needle showing above fabric determines length of quilting stitch.) Referring to **Fig. 18**, rock needle up and down, taking 3 - 6 stitches before bringing needle and thread completely through layers. Check back of quilt to make sure stitches are going through all layers. If necessary, make 1 stitch at a time when quilting through seam allowances or along curves and corners.

Fig. 18

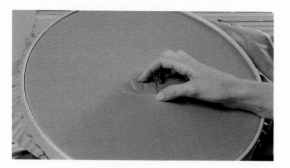

4. At end of thread, knot thread close to fabric and "pop" knot into batting; clip thread close to fabric.
5. Move hoop as often as necessary. Thread may be left dangling and picked up again after returning to that part of quilt.

MACHINE QUILTING METHODS

Use general-purpose thread in bobbin. Do not use quilting thread. Thread the needle of machine with general-purpose thread or transparent monofilament thread to make quilting blend with quilt top fabrics. Use decorative thread, such as a metallic or contrasting-color general-purpose thread, to make quilting lines stand out more.

Straight Line Quilting

The term "straight-line" is somewhat deceptive, since curves (especially gentle ones) as well as straight lines can be stitched with this technique.
1. Set stitch length for 6 - 10 stitches per inch and attach walking foot to sewing machine.
2. Determine which section of quilt will have longest continuous quilting line, oftentimes area from center top to center bottom. Roll up and secure each edge of quilt to help reduce the bulk, keeping fabrics smooth. Smaller projects may not need to be rolled.
3. Begin stitching on longest quilting line, using very short stitches for the first 1/4" to "lock" quilting. Stitch across project, using 1 hand on each side of walking foot to slightly spread fabric and to guide fabric through machine. Lock stitches at end of quilting line.

4. Continue machine quilting, stitching longer quilting lines first to stabilize quilt before moving on to other areas.

Free Motion Quilting

Free motion quilting may be free form or may follow a marked pattern.
1. Attach darning foot to sewing machine and lower or cover feed dogs.
2. Position quilt under darning foot. Holding top thread, take 1 stitch and pull bobbin thread to top of quilt. To "lock" beginning of quilting line, hold top and bobbin threads while making 3 to 5 stitches in place.
3. Use 1 hand on each side of darning foot to slightly spread fabric and to move fabric through the machine. Even stitch length is achieved by using smooth, flowing hand motion and steady machine speed. Slow machine speed and fast hand movement will create long stitches. Fast machine speed and slow hand movement will create short stitches. Move quilt sideways, back and forth, in a circular motion, or in a random motion to create desired designs; do not rotate quilt. Lock stitches at end of each quilting line.

MAKING A HANGING SLEEVE

Attaching a hanging sleeve to back of wall hanging or quilt before the binding is added allows project to be displayed on wall.
1. Measure width of quilt top edge and subtract 1". Cut piece of fabric 7"w by determined measurement.
2. Press short edges of fabric piece 1/4" to wrong side; press edges 1/4" to wrong side again and machine stitch in place.
3. Matching wrong sides, fold piece in half lengthwise to form tube.
4. Follow project instructions to sew binding to quilt top and to trim backing and batting. Before Blindstitching binding to backing, match raw edges and stitch hanging sleeve to center top edge on back of quilt.
5. Finish binding quilt, treating hanging sleeve as part of backing.

6. Blindstitch bottom of hanging sleeve to backing, taking care not to stitch through to front of quilt.

7. Insert dowel or slat into hanging sleeve.

BINDING

Binding encloses the raw edges of quilt. Because of its stretchiness, bias binding works well for binding projects with curves or rounded corners and tends to lie smooth and flat in any given circumstance. Binding may also be cut from straight lengthwise or crosswise grain of fabric.

MAKING CONTINUOUS BIAS STRIP BINDING

Bias strips for binding can simply be cut and pieced to desired length. However, when a long length of binding is needed, the "continuous" method is quick and accurate.

1. Cut square from binding fabric the size indicated in project instructions. Cut square in half diagonally to make 2 triangles.

2. With right sides together and using ¹/₄" seam allowance, sew triangles together (**Fig. 19**); press seam allowance open.

Fig. 19

3. On wrong side of fabric, draw lines the width of binding as specified in project instructions, usually 2¹/₂" (**Fig. 20**). Cut off any remaining fabric less than this width.

Fig. 20

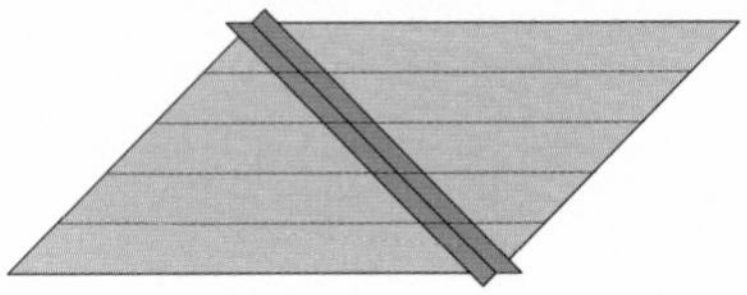

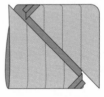

4. With right sides inside, bring short edges together to form tube; match raw edges so that first drawn line of top section meets second drawn line of bottom section (**Fig. 21**).

Fig. 21

5. Carefully pin edges together by inserting pins through drawn lines at point where drawn lines intersect, making sure pins go through intersections on both sides. Using ¹/₄" seam allowance, sew edges together; press seam allowance open.

6. To cut continuous strip, begin cutting along first drawn line (**Fig. 22**). Continue cutting along drawn line around tube.

Fig. 22

7. Trim ends of bias strip square.
8. Matching wrong sides and raw edges, press bias strip in half lengthwise to complete binding.

MAKING STRAIGHT-GRAIN BINDING

1. Cut lengthwise or crosswise strips of binding fabric the determined length and the width called for in project instructions. Piece strips to achieve necessary length.
2. Matching wrong sides and raw edges, press strip(s) in half lengthwise to complete binding.

ATTACHING BINDING WITH MITERED CORNERS

1. Beginning with 1 end near center on bottom edge of quilt, lay binding around quilt to make sure that seams in binding will not end up at a corner. Adjust placement if necessary. Matching raw edges of binding to raw edge of quilt top, pin binding to right side of quilt along 1 edge.
2. When you reach first corner, mark ¹/₄" from corner of quilt top (**Fig. 23**).

Fig. 23

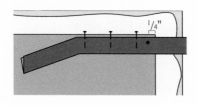

3. Beginning approximately 10" from end of binding and using ¹/₄" seam allowance, sew binding to quilt, backstitching at beginning of stitching and at mark (**Fig. 24**). Lift needle out of fabric and clip thread.

Fig. 24

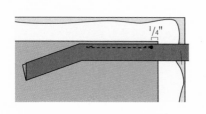

4. Fold binding as shown in **Figs. 25–26** and pin binding to adjacent side, matching raw edges. When reaching the next corner, mark ¹/₄" from edge of quilt top.

Fig. 25   Fig. 26

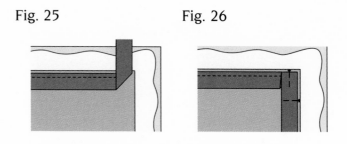

5. Backstitching at edge of quilt top, sew pinned binding to quilt (**Fig. 27**); backstitch at the next mark. Lift needle out of fabric and clip thread.

Fig. 27

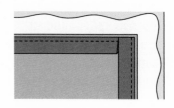

6. Continue sewing binding to quilt, stopping approximately 10" from starting point (**Fig. 28**).

Fig. 28

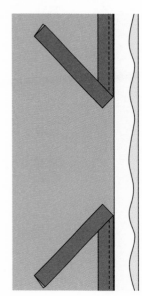

7. Bring beginning and end of binding to center of opening and fold each end back, leaving a $\frac{1}{4}$" space between folds (**Fig. 29**). Finger-press folds.

Fig. 29

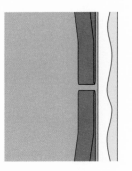

8. Unfold ends of binding and draw a line across wrong side in finger-pressed crease. Draw a line through the lengthwise pressed fold of binding at same spot to create a cross mark. With edge of ruler at marked cross, line up 45° angle marking on ruler with one long side of binding. Draw a diagonal line from edge to edge. Repeat on remaining end, making sure that the two lines are angled the same way (**Fig. 30**).

Fig. 30

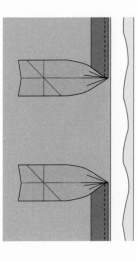

9. Matching right sides and diagonal lines, pin binding ends together at right angles (**Fig. 31**).

Fig. 31

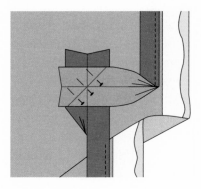

10. Machine stitch along diagonal line, removing pins as you stitch (**Fig. 32**).

Fig. 32

11. Lay binding against quilt to double-check that it is correct length.
12. Trim binding ends, leaving $\frac{1}{4}$" seam allowance; press seam open. Stitch binding to quilt.
13. If using $2\frac{1}{2}$"w binding (finished size $\frac{1}{2}$"), trim backing and batting a scant $\frac{1}{4}$" larger than quilt top so that batting and backing will fill the binding when it is folded over to quilt backing.

14. On 1 edge of quilt, fold binding over to quilt backing and pin pressed edge in place, covering stitching line (**Fig. 33**). On adjacent side, fold binding over, forming a mitered corner (**Fig. 34**). Repeat to pin remainder of binding in place.

Fig. 33   Fig. 34

15. Blindstitch binding to backing, taking care not to stitch through to front of quilt.

HAND STITCHES
BLIND STITCH
Come up at 1, go down at 2, and come up at 3 (**Fig. 35**). Length of stitches may be varied as desired.

Fig. 35

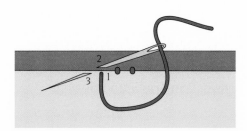

CHAIN STITCH
Come up at 1 and go down again at 1 to form a loop. Keeping loop below point of needle, come up at 2 and go down again at 2 to form second loop (**Fig. 36**). Continue making loops or "chain" until reaching end of line. Tack last loop (**Fig. 37**).

Fig. 36   Fig. 37

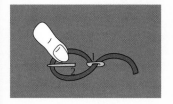
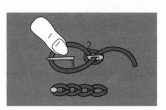

FRENCH KNOT
Follow **Figs. 38-41** to complete French Knots. Come up at 1. Wrap thread twice around needle and insert needle at 2, holding end of thread with non-stitching fingers. Tighten knot then pull needle through, holding floss until it must be released.

Fig. 38   Fig. 39   Fig. 40   Fig. 41

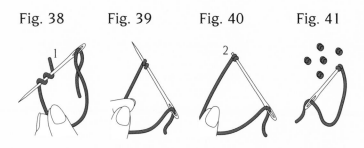

RUNNING STITCH
The running stitch consists of a series of straight stitches with the stitch length equal to the space between stitches. Come up at 1, go down at 2, and come up at 3 (**Fig. 42**).

Fig. 42

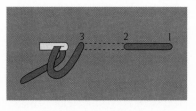

STEM STITCH
Come up at 1. Keeping thread below the stitching line, go down at 2 and come up at 3. Go down at 4 and come up at 5 (**Fig. 43**).

Fig. 43

Signing & Dating
YOUR QUILT

A completed quilt is a work of art and should be signed and dated. There are many different ways to do this and numerous books on the subject. The label should reflect the style of the quilt, the occasion or person for which it was made, and the quilter's own particular talents. Following are suggestions for recording the history of the quilt or adding a sentiment for future generations.

- Embroider the quilter's name, date, and any additional information on quilt top or backing. Matching floss, such as cream floss on white border, will leave a subtle record. Bright or contrasting floss will make the information stand out.

- Make label from muslin and use permanent marker to write information. Use different colored permanent markers to make label more decorative. Stitch label to back of quilt.

- Use photo-transfer paper to add image to white or cream fabric label. Stitch label to back of quilt.

- Piece an extra block from quilt top pattern to use as label. Add information with permanent fabric pen. Appliqué block to back of quilt.

- Write message on appliquéd design from quilt top. Attach appliqué to back of the quilt.